369 0144743

2014

This book is to be returned on or before
the last date stamped below.

D1611990

Glenn Geher, PhD, is professor and chair of psychology at the State University of New York at New Paltz. He is also director of the university's interdisciplinary Evolutionary Studies program, which was recently, along with a sister program at Binghamton University, awarded a large grant from the National Science Foundation. Dr. Geher is a past president of the Northeastern Evolutionary Psychology Society, the world's second largest society dedicated to the study of human behavior from an evolutionary perspective. He has published 30 scholarly books, book chapters, and articles on evolutionary psychology, including *Mating Intelligence*, coedited with Geoffrey Miller. Dr. Geher also writes a popular blog for the international Evolutionary Studies Consortium, "Building Darwin's Bridges." He was awarded the SUNY New Paltz Alumni Association's Distinguished Teacher of the Year Award in 2007 as well as the SUNY Chancellor's Excellence in Teaching Award in 2008.

Evolutionary Psychology

101

Glenn Geher, PhD

SPRINGER PUBLISHING COMPANY
NEW YORK

Springer Publishing Company, LLC
11 West 42nd Street
New York, NY 10036
www.springerpub.com

Acquisitions Editor: Nancy S. Hale
Composition: Amnet

ISBN: 978-0-8261-0718-3
e-book ISBN: 978-0-8261-0719-0

Parts of Chapter 4 were adapted from my coauthored book, *Mating Intelligence Unleashed: The Role of the Mind in Sex, Dating, and Love,* published by Oxford University Press, with the expressed written consent of the publisher.

Parts of Chapter 9 were adapted from my 2006 article published in *Entelechy,* titled "An Evolutionary Basis to Behavioral Differences Between Cats and Dogs," with the expressed written consent of the editor.

Parts of Chapter 9 were adapted from my article "Evolutionary Psychology Is Not Evil!" published in *Psychological Topics,* with the expressed written consent of the editor.

Parts of Chapter 9 were adapted from my article "There Are No Evolved Behavioral Sex Differences in Humans Because I Want It That Way!" published in the *EvoS Journal* in 2010, with the expressed written consent of the editor.

13 14 15 16 / 5 4 3 2 1

The author and the publisher of this Work have made every effort to use sources believed to be reliable to provide information that is accurate and compatible with the standards generally accepted at the time of publication. The author and publisher shall not be liable for any special, consequential, or exemplary damages resulting, in whole or in part, from the readers' use of, or reliance on, the information contained in this book. The publisher has no responsibility for the persistence or accuracy of URLs for external or third-party Internet websites referred to in this publication and does not guarantee that any content on such websites is, or will remain, accurate or appropriate.

Library of Congress Cataloging-in-Publication Data

Geher, Glenn.
  Evolutionary psychology 101 / Glenn Geher, PhD.
    pages cm.—(Psych 101)
  Includes bibliographical references and index.
  ISBN 978-0-8261-0718-3 (print edition : alk. paper)—ISBN 978-0-8261-0719-0 (e-book)
1. Evolutionary psychology.   I. Title.
  BF698.95.G44 2014
  155.7—dc23   2013026820

Special discounts on bulk quantities of our books are available to corporations, professional associations, pharmaceutical companies, health care organizations, and other qualifying groups. If you are interested in a custom book, including chapters from more than one of our titles, we can provide that service as well.

For details, please contact:
Special Sales Department, Springer Publishing Company, LLC
11 West 42nd Street, 15th Floor, New York, NY 10036-8002
Phone: 877-687-7476 or 212-431-4370; Fax: 212-941-7842
E-mail: sales@springerpub.com

Printed in the United States of America by Gasch Printing.

For Kathy, my life's solid rock.
And for Andrew and Megan—who make each day
shine like the sun.

Contents

CONTENTS

Preface

ince its emergence in the late 1980s and early 1990s, the field of evolutionary psychology has captured the imaginations and passions of scholars and laypeople across the world. Often peppered with a dash of controversy, this approach to psychology may be seen as having more potential than any other area of the behavioral sciences to help us understand who we really are.

The basic claims of evolutionary psychologists are, in fact, modest when one considers that they are rooted in the highly accepted premises of modern evolutionary theory. At its core, evolutionary psychology is an approach to human behavior that takes evolutionary theory into account. Often, this means that behavioral patterns are examined in terms of how such patterns might have provided survival and/or reproductive benefits to our ancestors in the African savanna. For example, our preferences for sweet foods and fatty meats seem to tell of a time in human evolution when famine was common, and having a preference for fatty meats would have encouraged early hominids to make food choices that would have provided them an edge in the competition to survive. We now know these same food preferences well—as the preferences that lead to epidemic rates of obesity under the decidedly nonfamine conditions that typify modern societies.

In addition to studying psychological processes that clearly lead to survival, evolutionary psychologists are interested in processes that may lead to reproductive benefits—sometimes even at a cost to survival. In fact, this broad mechanism of evolutionary change, referred to as *sexual selection*, may well be the dominant force in helping us understand many uniquely human characteristics, such as our capacity for language, art, and music. In a recent exploration of male English poets, Dan Nettle found that those with poems rated highest in quality had significantly more sex partners than those poets whose work was just so-so (Nettle & Clegg, 2006). If evolution is all about survival, why do people spend countless hours writing novels, learning instruments, and climbing the world's highest peaks? A rich body of literature in evolutionary psychology provides important insights into the role of sexual selection in having shaped the human mind.

Beyond addressing primary mechanisms of evolution as they pertain to human behavior, this book will summarize current research on many of the important content areas that have been elucidated by the work of evolutionary psychologists. These areas include child development, courtship, intrasexual competition, sex, pair-bonding, parenting, aggression, and altruism—all areas of human functioning that have been greatly illuminated by modern evolutionary psychology. These chapters provide a summary of how these domains of human functioning have been studied by evolutionary psychologists.

Given this area's penchant for getting people to think deeply about who we are, a final section of this book deals with applications of evolutionary psychology to many important personal and social issues. This section also addresses content regarding the many controversies that surround this field. Further, a final chapter addresses thoughts about the future of evolutionary psychology. As stated in Garcia et al. (2011), the future of evolutionary psychology is unclear. One possible future for this field is that it connects the islands of the "Ivory Archipelago" (Wilson, 2007) with its powerful framework and its tendency to cut across traditional academic boundaries. On the other hand, as challenges to the field show up repeatedly in scholarly circles, evolutionary psychology may be on a course toward increased controversy and intellectual alienation. This book ends with a discussion of the possible future of evolutionary psychology.

Acknowledgments

n 2009, Scott Barry Kaufman, my long-time collaborator, coauthor, and long-lost other brother, talked with me about this exciting new series being published by Springer—the Psychology 101 Series—and he talked about this really cool guy, James C. Kaufman (no immediate genetic relation), who was editing the series and whom Scott knew from graduate school at Yale. "Glenn, you've got to write *Evolutionary Psychology 101!* I spoke with James about it and he's psyched about the idea!" I like how Scott operates! I want to give him huge thanks for helping initiate the process that led to the book you now hold in your hands.

So Scott introduced me to the good James C. Kaufman, who immediately struck me as just as positive, forward-thinking, and resourceful as Scott led me to believe. James put me in touch with Springer editor Nancy S. Hale, and soon thereafter, this book got off the ground. Both James and Nancy have shown the kind of supportive and clear guidance that typifies the best of collaborators on any project. I am deeply appreciative of their efforts.

My interest in evolutionary psychology emerged based on an undergraduate class I took on animal behavior in the psychology department at the University of Connecticut in 1990, taught by Benjamin Sachs. This course was amazing—it was the first and only course I took as an undergraduate that made me see the interrelationship between many disparate phenomena. Why do South American coqui frogs call the way they do? Why are male elephant seals so much larger than their female counterparts? Why do female rats seem to try to physically prevent males from sexual access, even during the peak of their ovulatory cycle? It was amazing how the evolutionary perspective helped us understand all these phenomena within a single framework. After I took that course, Dr. Sachs let me work in his rat lab, focusing on the mating behavior of rats. Without question, it was these experiences that started my thinking on how evolution holds the key to understanding what behavior is all about. Many thanks, Dr. Sachs!

In graduate school at the University of New Hampshire (UNH), my two advisers, Jack Mayer and Becky Warner, played significant roles in helping me develop as a social scientist. Neither scholar is an evolutionary psychologist per se, but both were highly supportive of my interest in evolutionary psychology, and my ability to integrate evolutionary-based concepts into my research was fostered as a result. Many thanks to Jack and Becky, who strongly supported my intellectual trajectory!

Also while I was in graduate school, it's noteworthy that David Buss, then at the University of Michigan, came to UNH to give a talk on his then-new book, *The Evolution of Desire*. Like me, he was studying issues of human intimate relationships—but he called it "human mating"—and he focused fully on evolutionary accounts in explaining his data and research in general. That was it for me—I was hooked. His vision and approach to psychology allowed me to see for the first time how the integrative approach that Ben Sachs took in the study of nonhumans could be applied to human behavior. That's when I formally realized that *evolutionary psychology* is, for me, the only way to go!

My wife, Kathy, has been not only supportive in discussing topics related to evolutionary psychology but she's also consistently been supportive of this book project, allowing me to grab pockets of time here and there to write. Thanks, Kathy, for always being so supportive and awesome! Our life is a balancing act—and you make all the great things we have possible.

Our kids, Megan and Andrew, also have been supportive—and lots and lots of fun! As a regular at the NorthEastern Evolutionary Psychology Society (NEEPS), Megan, my best buddy, has always been helpful in discussing this field with me and has played a major role in helping me edit the references! I also note that most of this book was written under extremely fun conditions—in our Wii room while sitting on a beanbag chair next to my son and best friend, Andrew, while he mastered levels on Super Mario Bros.!

This project, like any large project, is always the result of lots of blood, sweat, and elbow grease, and the support of the many people in my life has been pivotal in allowing me to write this book on top of everything else I've got going on at any given time. I'd like to specifically acknowledge the help of Dan Lynn, biology teacher extraordinaire, whose comments on early drafts of this book helped me very much in keeping things on task—thanks, Dan! Further, the group who has supported me through this project includes the great undergraduate students at SUNY New Paltz, the incredible Evolutionary Psychology Lab at New Paltz, the folks associated with the Evolutionary Studies (EvoS) program, my colleagues in the psychology department, the always-awesome NEEPS, and more. In particular, huge thanks go to star graduate student and assistant, Briana Tauber, for extraordinary editorial support for this project and for helping with so many of the details that relate to pretty much all of my work! Largely due to the fact that I'm surrounded by a battery of smart, helpful, and community-oriented people in multiple life domains have I been able to produce this book—and I truly appreciate having such wonderful people in my life.

Evolutionary
Psychology
101

Introducing Evolutionary Psychology

E volutionary psychology is, essentially, the application of evolutionary principles to questions of human behavior. Soon after Darwin discovered the principles of biological evolution, he started to think and write about how the principles of natural selection can help us understand the nature of behavior—beyond exclusively applying evolution to understanding physical features of life forms. In his books on this topic, including *The Expression of Emotion in Man and Animals* (1872), he considered behavioral patterns of humans and other animals as serving ultimate functions related to facilitating reproductive success. Behavior and underlying psychological processes are likely the result of evolutionary forces, such as natural selection.

This idea stewed within academic circles for decades. This introductory chapter discusses the history of evolutionary thinking within the behavioral and social sciences, as well as the basic principles of evolution that are fundamental to understanding the nature of human behavior.

What Is Evolutionary Psychology?

KEY TERMS

- Adaptation
- Cultural evolution
- Environment of evolutionary adaptedness (EEA)
- Evolutionary mismatch
- Genetic drift
- Meme
- Multilevel selection
- Natural selection
- Organic evolution
- Reproductive success
- Selfish gene
- Sexual selection
- Sociobiology
- Spandrel
- Trade-off

et's start with a puzzle. Think about how the following phenomena are connected to one another:

- Emperor penguins have been shown to shove a fellow emperor penguin into the water to test if seals or other predators are in the area (Marchand & Higgins, 1990).
- The seed of a maple tree comes in a tidy package that resembles an outstanding helicopter blade—and in early spring, the wind can carry these seeds quite a distance (Darke, 2002).
- The single best statistical predictor of filicide (killing one's child) in humans is status as a step-parent (rather than as a biological parent; Daly & Wilson, 1988).
- When a male lion takes over the harem of another male, he kills all cubs sired by the ousted male. Next, each adult female quickly copulates with the new male, often forcing abortions of fetuses sired by the first male (Packer & Pusey, 1983).
- The human expression of happiness, a smiling face, is interpreted unmistakably and accurately across the globe—regardless of the cultural background of the person smiling or of the person rating the smile (Ekman & Friesen, 1968)

So here we have it. On the surface, these phenomena are strikingly unrelated. Penguins pushing each other. Maple seeds falling in spring. Parents killing their children. Lionesses copulating with murderous lions. The universal nature of the human smile. What's going on here?

Clearly, the nature of this book gives away part of the answer. Evolution sheds important light on all these phenomena. What's amazing about evolutionary psychology, compared to other approaches to understanding the human mind and behavior, is that the evolutionary approach has the power, as you'll soon see, to integrate phenomena across any and all behavioral domains—and even across species.

Let's look at how this conception of evolutionary psychology (and of evolutionary theory more generally) helps us understand our puzzle. A core idea in evolutionary theory pertains to *reproductive success* (RS). This is the idea that life forms evolved a host of features that facilitate the ability of the organism to reproduce. From this perspective, survival is actually a detail. Survival, from the perspective of evolution, is a tool that ultimately works toward reproduction (the reasoning behind this will be elucidated as this chapter progresses). A simple understanding of evolution is the idea that organisms that exist *must exist* because their ancestors had features that led to RS (otherwise the organism in question couldn't exist). So any features of a species that are *species typical* may well have the *ultimate purpose* of increasing RS.

This stripped-down account of evolution is actually remarkably powerful. Why do emperor penguins sometimes shove conspecifics (members of their own species) to a bloody death into the teeth of killer seals? Well, if you're the penguin who shoves, you learn some extraordinary information that will be very helpful in your own survival and ultimate RS. In terms of the maple seeds, think about optimal dissemination of one's genes. The helicopter design of the seed pod in maples, loved by children across continents, was clearly shaped by millions of years of evolution to help trees disseminate their seeds broadly—increasing the RS of the trees themselves. Once we think of organisms as designed to increase their own RS, it becomes immediately apparent that step-parents would be more likely to harm offspring than biological parents (it doesn't help a step-parent's RS to invest time and energy into the offspring of a conspecific). Similarly, lions that kill the cubs of male competitors seem to be acting out an evolutionary design that facilitates their own RS at the cost of the RS of the competing male. And why is smiling so universally understood in our species? Because accurate detection of emotion is a core feature of succeeding in the social worlds in which we find ourselves as humans—and succeeding socially, in a highly social species such as ours, is ultimately a core feature of succeeding in the evolutionary currency of RS.

WHAT IS EVOLUTION?

Before we get into the details of how evolution pertains to human behavior and the human mind, we need to define how the term *evolution* is used in this book. Importantly, note that evolution is actually broader than you might think. People typically see *evolution* in terms of *evolution of life*—or how organisms (such as you or me) came to exist across millions of generations and billions of years. Granted, that is pretty broad. However, the evolution of life is actually a subset of the broader concept of evolution proper. Evolution pertains to how any kind of entity changes across time. Across time, entities change. Some aspects of entities remain unchanged. Some changes are dramatic (such as the change from a caterpillar to a butterfly—a full metamorphosis that happens in a matter of weeks).

Importantly, life forms are not the only kinds of entities that evolve. This book evolved dramatically—from an idea, to a written proposal, to a rewritten proposal, to a draft, to a second draft, to a third draft, and so forth. In the 1980s, personal computers were rare, and they could handle only a very small number of computations relative to what exists now. In the 1990s, personal computers became more common and advanced, and the Internet came on the scene in a big way. Between 2000 and 2010, computers become commonplace, and advances in speed and abilities of personal computers were extraordinary. Various satellite technologies (cell phones, Facebook, etc.) emerged in a dramatic fashion. These days, it's clear that technology continues to advance at a rate that is hard to grasp for minds like ours. Technology evolves.

Much of this chapter will be about defining evolution. Perhaps the most basic and applicable definition came from renowned biologist George Williams, who wrote that evolution is nothing more than a "statistical bias in the rate of perpetuation of alternatives" (1966, p. 22). In short, alternative forms of any kind of entity exist. Some are, for any number of reasons, more likely to replicate than others. By definition, these "likely-to-replicate" forms exist in relatively high frequencies in the future—and that's it. As you can see, this conception of evolution is bigger than life itself!

Darwin's Big Idea

Born on February 12, 1809, Charles Darwin was destined for greatness. His interest in the natural world started in his childhood in England. Having been raised in a family with a great deal of money and a deep history of academic curiosity, Darwin was well positioned to discover the basic principles of evolution. Importantly, Darwin wasn't the first to discover evolution itself (the idea that species may have evolved from prior species with similar qualities, and that multiple life forms may have a common ancestor). Several naturalists before him had suggested this kind of thing. Rather, in his detailed and comprehensive account of the origins of life, *On the Origin of Species by Means of Natural Selection, or the Preservation of Favoured Races in the Struggle for Life* (Darwin, 1859), Darwin proposed a likely *mechanism* of evolution of life. In other words, he articulated *how* evolution was possible.

Importantly, Darwin's great contribution to our understanding of the universe primarily focuses on the evolution of life (or *organic evolution*)—but, clearly, the basic premises he articulated are applicable more broadly. In fact, the basic ideas of evolution are fully applicable across all areas studied within any university (see Wilson, 2007).

In any case, we can thank Darwin for helping us understand the primary mechanisms underlying evolution. The primary mechanism that he described was *natural selection*—which, like most solid academic terms, actually means what it says, as we'll soon see.

In his famous journey around the world as the naturalist on the HMS *Beagle*, Darwin explored the flora (plant life) and fauna (animal life) up and down South America and, famously, into the Galapagos Islands. Darwin had many great insights—but his big idea had to do with connections across everything he saw. How do the beaks of the finches of the Galapagos Islands, the courtship behaviors of the blue-footed boobies, the fossilized remains of ancient glyptodonts, and the cultural features of nonwesternized societies in the Amazon forests relate to one another? Darwin's big idea was that they all related to one another strongly, and that all these life forms likely came from some common ancestor. Now that's a big idea!

The specific mechanism of evolution that hit Darwin in his journey was that of *natural selection*—the idea that features of organisms that are *adaptive*, or that somehow help with the survival and/or reproduction of the organism, are selected and retained as part of the species. So these features that help an organism survive and reproduce are selected naturally. While we'll get into the details of natural selection later in this chapter, this is pretty much it.

Further, and importantly, Darwin understood the idea of *fitness*—how well (in Darwinian terms) the features of an organism *fit* the environment of an organism. This idea is best explicated with Darwin's observations regarding the beaks of the finches of the Galapagos Islands. What struck him were the important similarities and differences across the different species he found there. While the many different species of finches he found were similar to one another in most morphological (bodily) features, he noted pronounced differences in the beaks of the different species. The beaks of finches on the rocky coast were long (like beaks of many shore birds), ideal for picking out food in crevices between rocks. Beaks of finches in the inland rain forests were shorter and stronger, ideal for picking insects from the bark of trees, and so forth. The beaks of these different finches *fit* their particular environments. This is a prime example of Darwin's use of the term *fitness*. We'll turn back to Darwin's ideas on fitness when we consider the details of natural selection later in this chapter. For now, realize that Darwinism is extremely *environmentalist*—that is, this perspective underscores the nature of an organism's environment as shaping the nature of that organism and its species.

SELFISH GENE

In 1976, Richard Dawkins, perhaps the world's best-known living scientist, published *The Selfish Gene*—a landmark book that made Darwin's ideas accessible to a broad audience, and one that set the stage for the field of evolutionary psychology—and the idea that behavioral patterns (like any morphological features) are primarily the result of evolutionary forces.

Importantly, in this treatise on evolution, Dawkins didn't refute anything that Darwin said. In fact, he comes across as a full-blooded Darwinist. What was great about this book was how accessible it was for a (then) modern audience—and the seeds planted by this book have played an important role in influencing so much of modern-day evolutionary psychology. In essence, Dawkins' book was a fantastic summary and presentation of Darwin's ideas on the nature of evolution.

The concept of the *selfish gene* is the idea that genes are the basic replicating unit of all life forms, and that we can understand the nature of life by understanding conceptual properties of genes. Genes code for specific organisms—and through reproduction, genes replicate. So Dawkins' angle addresses the issue of which genes replicate and which do not. In his reasoning, Dawkins concludes that good replicator genes have the qualities of:

- Fecundity (being able to make a lot of replications of themselves in a lifetime)
- Longevity (being able to lead a long life, which increases replication [or reproducing] opportunities)
- Fidelity (being able to oversee the protein-creation process [or *RNA synthesis*—the specific task of genes] with accuracy, so that the genes of the next generation contain few copying errors)

Given a broader perspective on evolution, we can actually take this angle beyond genes and apply it to any replicating entities. Replicating entities that reproduce a lot, that last for a long time, and that replicate accurately will, by definition, be more likely to exist in the future compared to alternative entities (in *gene terms*, variants or alternative forms are called *alleles*).

This is the basic idea of evolution. For this reason, it does not make sense to talk about evolution proper as *true* or *false*—by definition, logically, replicating entities will be more prevalent in the future than nonreplicating entities! It's this simple and elegant presentation of evolution that may serve as Dawkins' greatest scholarly contribution to the world.

The concept of the *selfish gene* is this same concept regarding replicating entities. The idea is that genes that code for qualities that facilitate their own replication are, by definition, more likely to exist in the future (and to come to characterize a particular species) compared with alleles or alternative genes. Thus, genes that *effectively lead to their own replication* (such as those that are *selfish*) are likely to be *selected* to exist in the future. This is what the word *selfish* means in the context of *The Selfish Gene*.

SPECIES FROM THE PERSPECTIVE OF EVOLUTIONARY PSYCHOLOGY

An important implication of Darwin's ideas (and Dawkins' summary of these ideas) pertains to the nature of species. Interestingly, the truly Darwinist understanding of the place of species in the broader landscape of evolution is perhaps the single most misunderstood concept in all of academia!

People often think that evolution is all about species. But it's not. Species exist—and they are the result of evolution—but, importantly, species are artifacts of evolution! Consider two different genes: one that has the effect of increasing the organism's ability to find a mate, and the other primarily devoted to the species. It doesn't help the organism find a mate, but it helps the organism work with conspecifics to help these conspecifics find mates. The first gene is for the good of the gene (via being for the good of the organism). The second is for the good of the species. All things equal, which gene is more likely to lead to having itself replicated? Well, the first gene is a good candidate for replication. It helps the organism itself mate and ultimately reproduce. The second one inhibits the organism from reproducing, but helps others in the species (who may or may not have this same allele) mate and reproduce. The second gene is less likely to actually get itself replicated into the future. In fact, it's very likely to lead to its own demise, as individuals with this variant of the gene are likely to not reproduce themselves and are likely to help others reproduce instead (likely with the other variant). You can see from this example how the first gene (that is *for the good of the individual*) is likely to be selected and to become part of the species. The second gene (that is *for the good of the species*) is actually not likely to become a species-typical gene!

In short, genes that come to typify a species are not genes that are primarily designed to help the species! Genes that are primarily designed to facilitate the RS of the individual are genes that come to typify a species. This is why emperor penguins have a behavioral propensity to push conspecifics into the water to test for predators—and why male lions kill the offspring of competing males when taking over a harem. These examples are cold, nasty, and unpleasant. Importantly, as you'll see in this book, human behavior only includes some of this kind of stuff! That said, it's important to understand this early on. Darwin talked about species, but evolution is not about species. Evolution is about the replication of qualities that benefit individuals, and species are borne of this process.

As such, phrases such as "for the good of the species" or "to the betterment of the species" totally and unequivocally mischaracterize anything that Darwin was trying to say. Evolutionary psychology is not about qualities that primarily benefit the human species.

In fact, with this all said, note that in evolutionary psychology, the issue of *species* is almost always irrelevant, especially if focusing exclusively on humans. Human evolutionary psychology focuses on the adaptations and psychological features of humans that are the products of evolutionary forces, with a large focus on how these adaptations helped our ancestors survive and reproduce, and with just about zero focus on how these adaptations helped our ancestors help the species of humans become successful as a species per se. As such, as I often tell my students, you might even want to avoid the word *species* in work that you present related to evolutionary psychology—it's almost always inappropriately placed and misguided given the nature of the field.

BASIC EVOLUTIONARY CONCEPTS: NATURAL SELECTION, HERITABILITY, MUTATION, ADAPTATION, FITNESS, AND REPRODUCTIVE SUCCESS

Any forces that lead entities to change over time are evolutionary in nature. The big one that made Darwin's legacy is *natural selection*, which, as briefly described prior, is simply the idea that some qualities of organisms are more likely to be selected by nature (naturally) than others. The best way to think about natural selection is mathematical. Imagine a population of individuals. Half of them have a gene that has the effect of increasing vigilance regarding predators. Such individuals with this variant of the gene are very wary of predators and tend to be overconcerned at times—jumping at moving shadows, and the like. The other members of the population do not have this same *predator vigilance* gene. They are all quite relaxed! Well, suppose there are actually many predators in the environment. Which kinds of individuals are likely to exist more in the future? Given the fact that there are real predatory threats, it's adaptive to be hyper-vigilant. As I've presented this scenario, the individuals with the *predator vigilance* gene are more likely to survive. Of course, being more likely to survive corresponds to being more likely to reproduce (as corpses are poor at reproducing). So let's think like geneticists and look ahead some generations. The next generation will likely have a higher proportion than the parent generation of individuals with the *predator vigilance* gene. Maybe it'll be 55% to 45% in terms of the ratio within the population. It could even be a smaller difference to still lead to important evolutionary change. Evolution of life forms takes many generations—and small differences in the RS rates of different alleles can lead to large changes over many generations.

Imagine things playing out in this same predator-rich environment 100 generations from now. Well, now we may actually see all organisms displaying the predator vigilance associated with that particular variant of that gene. The other form was not *selected naturally*, so it *bit the evolutionary dust*, as it were. The form of the gene associated with hypervigilance, on the other hand, is *naturally selected*—and, as stated prior, this phrase simply means what it says!

Natural selection is often discussed in terms of *heritability* or *heritable qualities of organisms*. These are qualities of organisms that are at least partly determined simply by genetics. Some aspects of organisms show strong heritability (e.g., the physical size of the organism relative to conspecifics) and other features show relatively low heritability (whether you're a Mets fan or a Yankees fan, for instance, is not likely coded in your genes). Natural selection tends to act on features of organisms that are at least partly heritable. Importantly, and interestingly, behavioral geneticists have found that most behavioral traits in humans (and other organisms) show some level of heritability (see Miller, 2007). So natural selection has a lot to work with, even when we're talking about human behavioral patterns.

Natural selection is also often discussed in terms of *mutations*, or random changes to genes in the replicating process. With any replicating process, there is the possibility of inaccuracy. If you photocopy an article, you may well have to do it a second time because you didn't have the paper placed correctly, the print was not dark enough, and so forth. The same is true of gene replication. An error in the process is referred to as a *mutation*. Ultimately, mutations that lead to some adaptive benefits to organisms are naturally selected, and it is by this process across many generations that new species evolve.

This said, evolutionary psychologists tend to focus less on mutations than other evolutionary scholars. This is largely because evolutionary psychologists study humans and we don't tend to study them in terms of future changes in our species (which would typically take thousands of generations). So evolutionary psychologists are aware of mutations (and as you'll see in some later sections, the topic of mutations does emerge somewhat in this field), but evolutionary psychology focuses little on speciation per se, and there's little focus on the concept of mutation as a result.

Other core concepts that relate to Darwin's ideas on natural selection pertain to *adaptation*, *fitness*, and *RS*. As you'll see, these concepts are all really different ways of conceptualizing natural selection. An *adaptation* is a feature of an organism that is a product of natural selection. It is a specific feature of an organism that has come to typify a species (or a significant subset of the species) because it helps members of the species overcome some important survival or reproduction-based hurdles and facilitates reproduction. In the prior example about hyper-predator-vigilance, we can say that this behavioral trait is an *adaptation*—a feature of the organism that facilitates survival and ultimately RS.

Fitness is, as shown before, a Darwinian term with a specific interpretation regarding the fit between the organism and the environment. Fitness exists when some feature of an organism fits well with the nature of the environment and, as a consequence, facilitates survival and/or reproduction. So a feature of an organism that *has* or that *increases* fitness (as it's often stated) is an adaptation. Adaptations increase fitness.

In the 1970s, renowned behavioral biologist Robert Trivers developed the term *reproductive success* to capture the importance of this concept in the landscape of evolution. RS is what it says—the ability of an organism to successfully reproduce. Focusing on RS makes it clear that evolutionary forces and natural selection are not ultimately about survival (although they are partly about survival). Ultimately, survival is only adaptive insofar as it ultimately increases RS. RS is evolution's bottom line.

Sexual Selection

In terms of a pure conception of natural selection, some concepts make intuitive sense. We can understand why arboreal (tree-dwelling) primates have particularly strong hand-grip strength (see Gallup & Frederick, 2010), for instance. If you live in the tall trees, it pays to be able to hold on well, and arboreal ancestors who had poor hand-grip strength did not reproduce as much as those with strong hand-grip strength.

Some features of organisms make less sense from a straight-forward natural-selection perspective. The particular feature that became famous for this idea is the peacock's tail. Large, gaudy, and conspicuous, this feature of peacocks makes little sense on the surface from a natural-selection perspective. Clearly, Asian tigers are more likely to see you and slow you down—and eat you—if you're carrying that kind of conspicuous baggage. Camouflage makes obvious evolutionary sense. The tail of the peacock does not, and this fact reportedly kept Darwin up at night!

At some point, Darwin figured out the riddle of the peacock's tail. Selection is not really about survival. Qualities that survive are less likely in the future compared with qualities that lead to reproduction! So he considered that perhaps the peacock's tail has some specific utility in the domain of reproduction—and, alas, it does. It turns out that peahens are more attracted to peacocks with brightly colored tails than to those with relatively dull plumage. So this conspicuous signal, which actually impedes survival (the big,

15

bright tail), was selected because it directly facilitates reproduction. All things equal, qualities that facilitate reproduction are more likely to be selected than qualities that only facilitate survival. As noted several times to this point, in evolutionary currency, reproduction trumps survival.

So Darwin's other big idea was that of *sexual selection*—the idea that qualities that facilitate reproduction in the mating domain may be selected simply because of their role in this particular domain, even if these same qualities hinder survival. Modern evolutionists talk of the related idea of the *handicap principle* (see Zahavi, 1975), suggesting that under some conditions, something that is obviously a hindrance to survival (e.g., the peacock's tail) can be attractive, based on the idea that if an individual is capable of doing pretty much everything anyone else can—even with this conspicuous handicap—this may be a sign that this individual has a particularly strong and mutation-free set of genes. This is clearly an interesting angle on how we think of the concept of sexiness.

Sexual selection comes in two varieties, each of which is crucial to understanding human evolutionary psychology. Some qualities of organisms evolved because they are attractive to potential mates (with the peacock's tail being the prime exemplar). This kind of sexual selection is referred to as *intersexual selection* (with "inter" meaning "between," so it's between the sexes).

Some qualities evolve because they help individuals of one sex outcompete members of their same sex in seeking sexual access to the opposite sex. This kind of selection is referred to as *intrasexual selection* (with "intra" meaning "within," so it's a selection process within members of the same sex). The enormous size of the Irish elk's antlers, which were up to 12 feet across from tip to tip in this extinct mammalian species, serves an oft-cited example of intrasexual selection. Bull elk tend to fight one another during mating season, with the winners gaining access to local females. They fight using their antlers. In such a scenario, larger antlers tend to lead to more success in the fighting arena, which leads to success in the mating domain. And, again with the idea of an evolutionarily shaped handicap, walking around with hundreds of pounds of antlers on your head is not really the most efficient design from a biomechanical perspective. The antlers of the Irish elk weren't selected because they facilitated survival—they were selected because they facilitated mating.

As we'll see as this book unfolds, both varieties of sexual selection play a major role in the field of evolutionary psychology.

EVOLUTIONARY MISMATCH

In studying the attachment between babies and their parents, John Bowlby (1969) took an evolutionary perspective. In his classic treatise of the field, Bowlby coined the term *environment of evolutionary adaptedness* (EEA). This concept pertains to the environmental conditions that typified the ancestors of a species, with the idea that organisms didn't evolve the features that they have to match their current environments. All organisms are the products of thousands of generations of selection prior to their existence. Yet evolution has no crystal ball. So the best that selection processes can do is provide an organism with adaptations that were helpful to its ancestors under whatever the ecological conditions were then—essentially making a probabilistic-based "guess" that the environment will be the same. Of course, environments change, but with no knowledge of if, how, and when such change will occur, preparing organisms for ancestral environments is essentially the best bet.

Usually this works out fine, but sometimes contexts change in a short amount of time and organisms find themselves in situations for which they are really not evolutionarily prepared. A famous example of this pertained to the sea turtles of Florida. For millions of years, sea turtles would come to the beaches of Florida to spawn and their hatchlings would head toward the sea—to live a life far away—and to return to Florida years later (much like New Yorkers!). It turns out that the way the young turtles knew to head toward the direction of the ocean was based on light glimmering off the sea at night. The sea beautifully reflects the light of the moon and the stars, and for millions of years, a simple algorithm of "head toward the light at night" allowed the turtles to effectively head toward the sea to pursue an effective life strategy. Well, then came Miami. Not built by the Onceler, but it's the same idea. Miami and the other big cities on the coast of Florida are filled with lots of bright lights at night, so this led to an ecological catastrophe for the sea turtles (see Schlaepfer, Runge, & Sherman, 2002). Shaped by evolution to head toward light at night, hatchlings started toward the highways and cities by the millions—meeting premature death instead of a long sea-dwelling life. This is still an issue today, addressed by several conservation societies.

This is a case of a mismatch between the current conditions that exist and the EEA of the sea turtles. Organisms evolve to match the qualities of the EEA, and when modern conditions don't match the EEA, there can be trouble.

Evolutionary psychology strongly relates to issues of the EEA for humans. Prior to the advent of agriculture about 10,000 years ago, humans did not stay put—they couldn't, as they had to follow the food. As such, they lived in small nomadic bands (with the best estimates of typical size being approximately 150; see Dunbar, 1992). Further, such clans of early *Homo sapiens* tended to include many families, so any individual in such a clan was likely related to a good proportion of the group. It was like this for millions of years for our species. The advent of agriculture led quickly to civilization, which then led quickly to a major EEA issue for our species. In westernized societies, people tend to live in large cities. They may encounter thousands of individuals in a day, with 99% of those individuals being strangers. The closest family member may be 500 miles away, and the most common form of communication may be texting via cell phone.

This is clearly a mismatch, and much of evolutionary psychology speaks to this mismatch. In the words of renowned evolutionists Leda Cosmides and John Tooby (1997, p. 85), "Our modern skulls house a Stone Age mind."

This mismatch leads to many modern problems of humanity. As an example, consider the fact that McDonald's is as popular as it is. Yet the food is famously bad in terms of nutritional value. How did this popularity come to be? From an evolutionary perspective, the answer pertains to the EEA. Under ancestral human conditions, drought in the African savanna was common—and with drought comes famine. If famine is common, then it makes sense that you'd try to get as much body fat on you as possible. However, high-fat and high-sugar-content foods were rare. All meat eaten by our ancestors was lean—there were no farms breeding fat pigs—as all animals were wild and athletic by necessity. A taste preference for high-fat and sugary foods under such conditions would clearly give an individual an advantage. As such, a preference would cause this individual to seek out high-fat and sugary foods, and consuming as much of these foods as possible (sound familiar?!) would be a great strategy given the overall scarcity of such foods and the constant fact of droughts in the environment. So these taste preferences would be selected, because individuals with these preferences would be better able to survive and, ultimately, reproduce to ultimately pass on these preferences to apes like ourselves! Our love of McDonald's (manifest by the billions and billions served) is the result of this mismatch between modern westernized societies and the human EEA. Clearly this fact results in such major health and societal outcomes as high rates of heart disease and type 2 diabetes. As you can see, evolutionary psychology provides a strong and powerful framework for understanding such important features of the human condition.

EVOLUTION AND BEHAVIOR:
THE BASIC PREMISE OF EVOLUTIONARY PSYCHOLOGY

If feminism is "the radical notion that women are people" (Kramare & Treichler, 1996), then evolutionary psychology is "the radical notion that human behavior is part of the natural world." From this perspective, it's very simple, and does not inherently yearn for controversy. The basic reasoning goes like this:

1. Organisms are the product of natural selection and other evolutionary forces.
2. Specific physical features of organisms are, thus, also the result of evolution.
3. The human nervous system is an important physical feature of our species (with the brain being the most intricate organ in the human body).
4. All behavior is the result of action of the nervous system.
5. Human behavior is, ultimately and importantly, the result of evolution.

That's it—that's evolutionary psychology in a nutshell!

Behavior, a broad and general concept that refers to all actions of organisms that possess nervous systems, is a crucial adaptation in evolutionary history. Before nervous systems existed, organisms could not move in reaction to stimuli in the environment (see Dawkins, 1976). A blade of grass moves slowly as it grows— but it is not able to dart out of the way of a predator such as a cow! Grasses have other adaptations (e.g., toxins) to address the "predator" issue.

At some point, some early organisms evolved a precursor to the nervous system that allowed for assessment of environmental stimuli and quick responses to such stimuli. This system was so adaptive that it replicated extensively. The human nervous system that allows me to type these words and that allows you to read them is one result of this extraordinary evolutionary story.

Behavior is clearly shaped by many factors. Evolutionary psychologists often refer to Niko Tinbergen's (1963) conception of *ultimate* versus *proximate* causes of behavior. The ultimate causes of a behavior pertain to its evolutionary (or phylogenetic) history, addressing questions such as *How did this behavior come to be? How was it adaptive? How did it confer reproductive benefits to individuals with such a behavioral quality?*

The proximate causes of behavior are relatively "immediate." For instance, activity in the amygdala in the lower part of the brain seems to be a precursor to aggressive behavior. So if we see a guy get out of control at the bar one night, we might think of this proximate cause—his amygdala has many neurons that are firing.

An evolutionist always sees all behaviors as caused by multiple factors, so in addition to the proximate cause described in this example (neuronal firing in the amygdala), we can also think about how male aggression has been retained and selected in our species—how has this pattern of behavior allowed our male ancestors to out-reproduce competitors? This is an *ultimate* question, and it goes back to an analysis of how this behavioral pattern (here, it looks like intrasexual competition, which may lead to increased mating opportunities) corresponds to average increases in RS.

Of course, there are likely additional proximate causes (perhaps someone pushed the guy in front of a large group, and this action served as a stimulus that triggered an aggressive response), and there may be additional ultimate causes (in addition to out-competing competitors, male aggression may actually, under some contexts, be attractive to potential mates).

The evolutionary approach to behavior is one that appreciates nuance and complexity! Further, it's a perspective that consistently incorporates environmental causes of behavior (e.g., ancestral contexts that selected for certain qualities) along with innate or internal causes of behavior (e.g., genes or brain systems that underlie behavior). Given this focus on both environmental and innate causes of behavior, coupled with a genuine focus on proximate and ultimate causes of behavior, evolutionary psychology is truly an approach to psychology that embraces both the *nature* and *nurture* side of the (somewhat silly) *nature/nurture* debate.

DRIFT, SPANDRELS, MULTILEVEL SELECTION, AND CULTURAL EVOLUTION

You'll see that the wording in this book tends to be careful to not conflate *evolution* with *natural selection*. In fact, for various reasons, it's important to discriminate *evolution* from *mechanisms that underlie evolutionary change*. Natural selection is a mechanism of evolution—it's not synonymous with evolution itself. The two forms of sexual selection that we described earlier in this chapter are also mechanisms of evolution, rather than evolution itself.

There are other mechanisms of evolution, and they all play roles in ultimately shaping patterns of human behavior! Evolutionary psychologists often tend to focus on natural and sexual selection. This is largely due to the fact that these forces are famously powerful, and a good working hypothesis regarding why some feature exists will typically start with questions of *adaptation* as a result of natural or sexual selection (see Wilson, 2007).

This said, there are other significant mechanisms that underlie evolution of human behavior, and a good evolutionary psychologist understands the nature of these mechanisms and how they may apply to human behavior. These additional mechanisms include:

A. Genetic Drift (or just *drift*). Drift is the idea that some genes become more prevalent in populations not because they lead to adaptive benefits relative to alleles, but simply because of happenstance regarding which genes were where when! Suppose you have an ancestral population of ungulates on the savanna. Two distinct coat patterns exist: one is tan with black spots, the other is tan with black stripes. Although these two different *phenotypes* (i.e., manifestations of specific genetic patterns, often referred to as *genotypes*) used to be equal in prevalence, a random flood several hundred years ago happened to wipe out one of the largest herds, and this herd happened to have a relatively high proportion of spotted animals. For this reason primarily, striped coats tend to dominate. There was nothing adaptive about the striped coat relative to the spotted coat. Due to somewhat random and uncontrollable factors, things just drifted this way.

B. Spandrels (or evolutionary by-products). The renowned paleontologist, Stephen J. Gould (1980), was famous for taking an antiadaptationist stance regarding much of evolution. Each adaptation, he argued, brings along several by-products that come to typify a species (just as the adaptations do), but that have no reproductive benefits—they just come along for the ride. In architecture, a term for such a feature is a *spandrel*. This is the space that exists under an arch. If you create, for instance, a bridge with several arches, each arch helps support the bridge. A by-product of this is the fact that you have several spandrels, and they may be used by various organisms for all kinds of purposes (such as nests for birds).

With this reasoning in mind, Gould warned evolutionary psychologists of being *hyperadaptationist* in their approach. While most evolutionary psychologists agree that adaptations are the primary result of evolution, Gould warns folks to think otherwise. For instance, he and others (e.g., Pinker, 1999) argue that our ability to read is not something that was selected because it gave our ancestors reproductive benefits. Pinker argues that the written word was actually developed by people well after the human brain evolved its capacity for language and higher-order cognition. So reading is an essential part of modern humans, but it's, according to Gould and Pinker, a by-product of language-related adaptations—not an adaptation per se. As evolutionists, we need to always keep Gould's point in the backs of our minds—and every now and again, it's good to argue against an adaptationist perspective by unleashing one's inner Gould!

C. Multilevel Selection. Another important concept to keep in mind regarding different kinds of evolutionary forces is Wilson's (2007) notion of multilevel selection. This is the idea that several evolutionary forces, at multiple levels, work simultaneously at a given time. A basic level of selection may be the gene (individuals, thus, may have adaptations that help them replicate their specific genes), but the individual him- or herself may be thought of as a separate unit on which evolutionary forces may act. Sometimes an individual may have a gene that is in the gene's interest, but not in the individual's interest (e.g., a gene that replicates in high frequencies by creating cancerous cells—these are cells that replicate a gene that is harmful to the individual).

In fact, Wilson would argue that selection is always acting at multiple levels—such levels including the genetic, cellular, organ-based, organism, kin group, social group, and other levels that ultimately surround an individual. Wilson has famously argued that there are many cases, particularly in humans (but in other species too), in which some feature has been selected because it is adaptive at one level (even if it is seems nonadaptive at a different level). As we'll see in Chapter 6, Wilson sees many traits that are fostered by religion (e.g., sacrificing your own interests for those of a neighbor) as having been selected not because they help individuals directly (self-sacrifice is, by definition, not helping oneself!), but as helping the group to which one belongs (with the idea that cultivating your group ultimately brings back benefits to the individual). If you're part of a large group of self-sacrificers, I'd say you can expect your broader group to thrive—particularly relative to a group of selfish jerks! It's not difficult to see how being in the self-sacrificer group can lead to ultimate benefits to the individual members of that group. Evolution takes place at multiple levels that surround an individual and his or her genes. Good evolutionary psychology takes this point deeply into account.

D. Cultural Evolution. In an important update to his classic book, *The Selfish Gene*, Dawkins (1989) created the term *meme*, which is, as he conceptualizes it, a cultural unit that has the capacity to be replicated—much like a gene. It's a piece of human culture or an idea. The beauty of this idea is that it still can be understood in terms of evolution! Some ideas catch on (think: cell phone!). Some ideas mutate (think about how modern dance music has its roots in the Bee Gees songs of the 1970s—it's true!). Some ideas never catch on (you may not remember the Beta videotape, which is proof in itself that it never caught on!).

In humans, cultural evolution is obviously huge and, importantly, it happens fast! Organic evolution takes thousands of generations to make important and observable changes in a population. However, in a very short amount of time, Justin Bieber's fun and poppy style took the world by storm, leading to *Bieber Fever* (which would easily have been observable by anthropologists from Mars [if there are any!]—especially with his 3-D movie that was released in 2011). Nothing shows the powerful and fast-acting nature of cultural evolution more than does Bieber Fever (and I haven't even gone into how his hairstyle alone captivated a generation! That hair is some meme!).

So when we're thinking about where human behavior originates, evolutionists will often start by thinking about adaptations shaped by natural and sexual selection. Given Darwin's big ideas, this is a powerful starting point. However, there are other important evolutionary forces at work as well—including drift, multilevel selection, and cultural evolution—along with the all-important concept of evolutionary by-products. Good evolutionary psychologists show a clear understanding of all these concepts and apply them to their understanding of human behavior when appropriate.

TRADE-OFFS

In the 1990s, I was fortunate to attend a lecture by the great evolutionist Noam Chomsky. During this presentation on the topic of the evolution of language, Chomsky addressed a major misconception about evolution. He essentially said that people often see natural selection as creating perfection—optimally designed living machines. In fact, Chomsky said (with some jest), "The last perfectly designed organism was the shark!" Two things about this joke: First off, it'd be helpful to know that sharks are ancient organisms, and the paleontological record shows little changes in many species of sharks across millions of years. Now that was a great design! Second, it's funny because none of us has ever met a perfect shark—sharks aren't perfect either!

Chomsky went on to note how evolution does *not* create perfect, optimal designs. That's not how it works. Evolutionary processes essentially select the best form (i.e., the most likely to replicate in the long run) of a discrete group of options. The human nervous system, for instance, is far from perfect. Mental illness and psychological problems that permeate many modern human societies can attest to this point. This said, the nervous system is amazing and clearly had qualities that allowed our ancestors with effective nervous systems to survive and reproduce relative to others. Still, evolution is not about the shaping of perfect qualities of organisms—it is about optimizing in light of alternatives that exist.

Evolutionary processes work in terms of trade-offs. Think about the importance of RS in an evolutionary framework. Given how important reproduction is, you'd think that individuals might start reproducing early. Twins might be more common.

Heck, triplets, quadruplets, and so on, might be the way to go. Maybe it would be optimal for people to have 2,000 offspring in a lifetime!

Well, every benefit comes with costs. For instance, reproducing too early in our species would have the cost of having parents be ill-prepared for child rearing. I can't really see a 5-year-old being a brilliant parent. Having a high number of offspring at a time leads to increased risks of death to both mother and child during childbirth, and so forth. With any benefit, there are trade-offs. There are always trade-offs with everything, and evolution, naturally, takes trade-offs into account.

SUMMARY: TURNING ON THE LIGHT

When Daly and Wilson (1988) examined patterns of homicide from an evolutionary perspective, their results shocked the academic world. Lots of folks had studied homicide before—it's an important social issue that we need to better understand and control. In short, homicide's bad! Before the seminal work of Daly and Wilson on this topic, it was poorly understood. Lots of little, isolated facts about the predictors of homicide had been studied. However, before an evolutionary approach was applied in this area, there was no roadmap. No set of guiding principles. No overarching set of guidelines to help with the research. Once Daly and Wilson examined this topic from an evolutionary perspective, it was as if someone had turned on the light.

Simply, these researchers expected that patterns of homicide would make evolutionary sense. One set of studies they conducted, for instance, focused on males' responses to sexual infidelity. In our species (as in other mammals), males can never be sure of paternity, and this fact should lead to several adaptations designed to help males reduce the likelihood that their partners are having someone else's baby. There are nasty sides to this approach. In a study of thousands of North American homicides,

Daly and Wilson found that approximately one third had to do with male sexual jealousy (with males killing their partner, the interloper [i.e., the other guy], or getting themselves killed along the way).

Here's another one. Daly and Wilson studied filicide (parents killing their own children). Obviously, this is disturbing. Prior research had uncovered some aspects of this phenomenon, but then Daly and Wilson "turned on the light" by using an evolutionary approach to understand this question. They found that, consistent with their predictions, step-parents were more than 100 times more likely to engage in filicide compared with biological parents. The single biggest predictor of engaging in filicide is status as a step-parent. This fact was completely missed by all researchers who examined filicide prior to this work by Daly and Wilson.

Human beings are the result of evolution. Our behavior is an important part of who we are. Evolutionary psychology is an approach to understanding human behavior by understanding our evolutionary past. The current movement in evolutionary psychology represents perhaps the single most important step in shaping the future of the behavioral sciences. By addressing the important behavioral domains examined by evolutionary psychologists, this book is designed to help "turn on the light" in shaping your understanding of the human mind and behavior. Enjoy the journey—and remember: Evolutionary psychology is the radical notion that human behavior is part of the natural world.

DISCUSSION/ESSAY EXERCISES

- Explain the idea of mismatch theory in terms of evolution. In your answer, explain the idea of the environment of evolutionary adaptedness (EEA). In your response, give examples of how modern human contexts mismatch ancestral contexts in important ways.

- Describe the notions of *adaptation, natural selection,* and *reproductive success* and the interrelatedness of these concepts. Also, describe the idea of a *spandrel,* and address how this concept serves as an important idea to consider in thinking about adaptations in evolutionary psychology.
- Explain the distinction between *organic evolution* and *cultural evolution.* In your answer, discuss how these concepts share similarities and differences. Also, provide at least one example of each kind of evolutionary process.
- Briefly describe Dawkins' (1976) notion of the selfish gene. In your answer, give an example of one kind of behavior—in any species—that explicates this concept. Finally, address the points of longevity, fidelity, and fecundity as they relate to the idea of gene replication.

Domains of Human Behavior Shaped by Evolution

By this point in the book, you can see that evolution relates to all aspects of human behavior. As such, all areas of psychology that are presented in a standard psychology curriculum can be examined in terms of evolutionary principles—evolutionary psychology is a general framework for understanding behavior as opposed to a particular area of psychology. Cognitive psychology, developmental psychology, social psychology, and so forth—all basic areas of psychology can benefit from taking an evolutionary approach.

Several specific domains of human behavior have been particularly illuminated by applications of the evolutionary approach. These domains are included in this section, organized in a way that speaks to basic aspects of human behavioral functioning. These include child development and parenting, issues of courtship and human mating, relationship and family issues, altruism and religious behavior, and aggression and its derivatives, such as war and murder. The chapters in this section summarize what evolutionary psychologists know regarding these aspects of humanity.

Evolution And Child Development: The Slowly Developing Ape

KEY TERMS

- Life history strategy
- Parental Investment Theory
- The relationship between parental investment and mating strategies
- Precocial species
- Altricial species
- Attachment theory
- Attachment behaviors
- Child mortality under nonwesternized conditions
- Education and play from an evolutionary perspective

- Evolutionary psychology and parenting
- Alloparenting
- Dunbar's number

ver see *Finding Nemo*? If so, recall that first scene. If not, here's a brief spoiler. A mother and father clownfish are happily anticipating the hatching of the thousands of fertilized eggs in their clutch, secured deeply near the bed of a coral reef in the South Pacific. Like many anticipatory parents, they are filled with positive emotions and expectations. Then the shark comes. It's nasty. He eats Mom, and every fertilized egg; except for one. You got it—that one's Nemo!

In the movie, Marlin, Nemo's caring and mildly imperfect father, shows consistent, deep, and genuine care for Nemo as the young male fish gets himself into all kinds of situations. Well, some of this is realistic—and some of it is Pixar. Yes, clownfish, like many species of fish, set a high number of potential offspring into the world, and the lion's share of those potential offspring die a standard Darwinian death. On the other hand, clownfish are not monogamous and clownfish dads don't really show the deep emotional affection for their offspring that Marlin experiences in the movie. It's a movie!

PARENTAL INVESTMENT THEORY

One of the single greatest feats in the life and behavioral sciences was Robert Trivers' (1972) articulation of Parental Investment Theory. A Harvard-trained biologist with an early focus on the behavior of various insect species, Trivers proved (and still proves) to be an extraordinary mind in the world of evolutionary studies. With a simple set of "I should have thought of that" ideas, parental investment theory has come to shape the nature of thousands of research studies across several areas of academic research.

In a nutshell, Trivers suggests that the required amount of parental investment in a given species will drive the nature of the behavioral strategies of that species. In particular, parental investment should shape the mating strategies demonstrated by each species. Consider clownfish. Where the creators of *Finding Nemo* get it wrong is exactly in the area of parental investment. In fact, clownfish, relative to lots of other species, do not invest that much in any particular offspring. During mating season, the female lays her many eggs, the male blasts them with sperm, some proportion are fertilized, a small proportion of the hatchlings live to swim, and the young ones spend their days of development swimming among the coral reef with no parental supervision. In fact, clownfish represent a classic instance of a low-parental-investment species—and this fact pertains directly to the short-term nature of clownfish mating. Courtship takes days rather than months or years. Egg fertilization is efficient with no romance. The relationship ends abruptly. Parental investment levels and mating strategies are, clearly in this case, interconnected.

King salmon found in the Pacific and the coastal waterways of Alaska and Canada have a story that is even more telling. These impressive beasts have a remarkable life history. They start as fertilized eggs many miles upstream from the ocean. Each egg is one of hundreds of thousands in a clutch. Predators are abundant, and immobile fertilized eggs are easy targets. The lucky ones hatch in the ocean, where they travel for miles and spend years. When they are sexually mature—often weighing in at over 20 pounds—they swim in droves back to their original stream—as far up as possible—avoiding grizzly bears as best they can. In a frenzy upstream, male and females seek one another out. An externally fertilizing species, like the lion's share of animals on this planet, the females release eggs and the males release sperm. Thousands of clutches of fertilized eggs, with each clutch comprised of hundreds of thousands of eggs, are released in a great biological lottery. Soon thereafter, the parents die—by design. Then the grizzly bears have a feast, and the life cycle continues this way as it has for thousands of generations.

Talk about low parental investment! Well, I suppose that the entire life of a salmon is really dedicated to the offspring—but the amount of investment provided to each potential offspring once they are created is clearly zero—and that goes for Mom and Dad. Oh, and, as predicted by Trivers' theory of parental investment, there is no monogamy in these creatures.

When required parental investment in a species is relatively low, short-term mating strategies prevail. When required parental investment in a species is high, long-term mating strategies come to typify the species. This rule, Trivers' great insight regarding parental investment, applies across species.

Robin fledglings develop from *embryo* to *juvenile with full flight* in a matter of weeks. This feat requires an extraordinarily fast metabolism. They have to eat a lot—and they can't exactly feed themselves. In this context, parental help beyond egg fertilization is essential. In line with Trivers' theory, robins (like many species of birds) are relatively monogamous.

So what of *Homo sapiens*? Are we an ape with offspring that require high levels of parental care to successfully develop and ultimately become a viable adult? Well, yeah! This answer is so obvious that it borders on the absurd. In humans, parental investment is high—period. We are a slowly developing ape. Humans aren't capable of reproduction until more than a decade into life. Required investment is high from the start. A developing embryo taxes a woman's body enormously—for nearly a full year. During this time, a woman experiences significant bodily changes, which often have adverse consequences for the mother (e.g., pregnancy sickness, increased risk of type 2 diabetes, increased risk of cardiac problems, etc.).

The costs of pregnancy in our species are enormous. And it doesn't end there. Childbirth is a major event—it also presents possible health-affecting issues to a mother. The greater the investment, the greater the parental costs. Further, our species is relatively *altricial*, meaning that our offspring are relatively helpless for an extended period (compared with species that are *precocial*, in which young are self-sufficient relatively early in life). Babies need a great deal of attention, including feeding. Under natural conditions, babies tend to nurse for more than 3 years. That's a lot of investment of time and energy! Once a human is weaned, parental costs hardly disappear. Toddlers can't exactly be expected to go out at 9:00 AM and come back at 5:00 PM. In our species, parental costs are high—and they remain high for an extended period. The help of multiple adults (which is represented by *bi-parental care*—parental costs typically shared by a mother and a father) is crucial in allowing human offspring to succeed.

Want to understand human psychology? Think about Trivers' great insight into the importance of parental investment in shaping the nature of any species—and think about how this fact has shaped who we are. There is no understating how significant this concept is in helping us understand who we are.

THE ASYMMETRICAL NATURE OF PARENTAL INVESTMENT IN HUMANS

A significant addendum to Trivers' theory of parental investment is found in the asymmetrical nature of parental investment across the sexes. In any sexually reproducing species, one sex tends to have higher required parental costs than the other sex. In mammals, defined as animals with internal fertilization, females tend to have naturally higher levels of required parental investment. And humans are no exception to this rule.

Women have higher parental costs than men from the outset. Biologically, sex is defined in terms of gamete size. The sex with the larger gamete is the female. In humans, a typical egg is much larger than a typical sperm cell. And the number of eggs that a female can produce is fixed. Thousands exist from birth in a young female. By puberty, the number is reduced. But, importantly, the number of eggs that a female will release during her lifetime is capped by issues of the ovulatory cycle, the onset of puberty, and the onset of menopause. During a female's reproductive years, she will typically release 12 eggs per year—and that's for about 35 years, give or take a bit. Further, under natural conditions, due to less than optimal nutrition and lack of advanced health care, women tend to ovulate about half as much as women who have these modern luxuries. So a good estimate of the number of eggs released by a typical ancestral woman is 210, and each egg holds all the nutrition needed for a developing embryo during the critical first days of existence.

Sperm are different. Functionally, a man's sperm count across life may as well be infinite. A single ejaculation can have more than a trillion sperm cells. Multiply that by the number of ejaculations that a male can have across his postpubescent life span. It's a lot! And what is the specific function of a sperm cell? The entire function is to activate and connect with an egg. Sperm cells are small and are designed for increased mobility—to outcompete other sperm cells in a Darwinian competition to facilitate future existence. They provide nothing in the way of nutrition for a developing embryo.

In terms of cost, eggs are rare and expensive, while sperm are plentiful and cheap. From the outset, costs of parenting are higher for females than for males. This asymmetry in parental investment across the sexes maps onto all aspects of sexual reproduction and child development in our species. To see this point, consider the following:

- Pregnancy has a high cost for females—not for males.
- Childbirth has a high cost for females—not for males.
- Nursing has a high cost for females—not for males.
- Caring for infants, babies, toddlers, and children disproportionately falls on the shoulders of females more than males—across all societies that have ever been studied.
- And so forth.

As Trivers' great insight into the importance of parental investment helps us understand the differences across species, this big idea allows us to, similarly, understand differences between males and females in a coherent and powerful way that, without an evolutionary framework, simply would be not attainable.

OUR CHILDREN ARE OUR WORLD— ATKINSON AND VOLK (2008)

Crimes against children bring about universal disgust. The evolutionary perspective helps us understand why this is so. Our children are the future of our entire genetic lineages rolled up into multicellular packages. Do what you want to me, but you'd best not mess with my kids!

In a shocking evolutionarily relevant exposé of the psychology of parenthood, Atkinson and Volk examined disturbing data. They studied child mortality rates—examining the rate of child mortality in many prewesternized societies—along with examining rates of child mortality in several prior cultures that have good documentation on this topic (such as in Japan about 1,000 years ago). All societies that they documented, importantly, were without modern westernized medicine, thus allowing for an assessment of the nature of child mortality under relatively natural human conditions. This method allows for a glimpse into the likely rates of child mortality during the environment of evolutionary adaptedness (EEA) for our species.

The data were remarkably clear and consistent. While some variability across samples existed, the variability was remarkably low. Typical rates of child mortality were, in other words, quite similar across the disparate populations being studied. The bottom line numbers follow: On average, approximately 50% of children (under natural conditions) do not see age 1, while 80% do not see age 18. Thus, most likely, during the EEA under which our minds evolved, 50% of babies died before a year and 80% of all children died before 18. Imagine how sad life must have been (and must be) under such conditions—hard to imagine, in fact.

Importantly, these conditions and realities must have characterized our ancestral conditions. Given how incredibly high parental costs are in our species and how incredibly altricial our young are, it makes sense that our parenting-psychology systems would have evolved to be extremely sensitive to dangers to our children. If you look at the extraordinary amount of focus and energy people place on the welfare of their children, you'll see that the evolutionary approach implied by Volk and Atkinson's (2008) work is an accurate characterization of the psychology of human parenting. The emotions and care that people invest in parenting are, without question, among the paramount aspects of being human. It is the evolutionary perspective that tells us why.

ATTACHMENT THEORY

Like the young of many altricial species, human beings develop attachments to early caregivers—mothers in particular. The foundational work in evolutionary psychology comes, in fact, from Attachment Theory developed by John Bowlby (1969), which suggests that the drive to form attachments early in life is an essential part of child development. Through crying, smiling, making eye contact, and being cute, our young emit various stimuli that we are designed to respond to—responding to such stimuli is in the evolutionary interest of any parent given that offspring are the true key to reproductive success.

As is true with many aspects of human behavior, the nature of attachment behaviors and outcomes is *conditional* and *ecologically sensitive*; that is, it seems that an optimal strategy of attachment to others is partly determined by one's early environment. If a child is held close and nurtured positively early on, a child is likely to develop a *secure* attachment style (see Ainsworth, Blehar, Waters, & Wall, 1978)—responding positively to others in a general sense and showing a genuine expectation of security in social contexts. On the other hand, if a child has had a harsh upbringing during early years, with little positive attention by primary caregivers during early childhood, such an upbringing may be a signal of an unstable future environment. In terms of *life history strategy*, which we've already discussed, a child in the latter scenario may be likely to develop a *fast* life history strategy. In the language of attachment theory, this would correspond to an *insecure* or, perhaps, *avoidant* attachment style. If early life conditions suggest harshness and unpredictability in social relationships, then an attachment style that does not lead to solid attachments with others may actually be adaptive (see Schmitt, 2008).

In short, the evolutionary approach provides a framework for understanding why attachments between children and parents are so critical in our species. This approach also provides a sense of how different patterns of attachment styles could co-exist as a function of differential ecological conditions in early childhood.

Play and Education

Renowned psychologist Peter Gray (2011) has spent a great deal of time studying child development across the school-age years. His work, rooted in an evolutionary perspective, focuses largely on the idea of mismatch. In particular, Gray focuses on education and how modern educational systems fare relative to what we know about human development and what we know about how education takes place in prewesternized contexts.

In his analysis, which is nearly parallel to Volk and Atkinson's (2008) analysis of child mortality rates, Gray has examined how education takes place in groups of people who are nomadic and whose lifestyles match those of our ancestors. What he has found is nothing short of eye-opening. In simple terms, the way we educate children in modern societies is weird! In nonwesternized societies, there are no lines between work, play, and education.

Children learn the ways of the group as a consequence of being part of the group day-in-and-day-out and playing with all the other children—all while learning specific tasks along the way. One of the most interesting things that Gray's research documents is the fact that, in such prewesternized conditions, most "education" takes place not from adults but, rather, from other children. The main teachers of children are other children, often children who are slightly older. Gray refers to this phenomenon as "scaffolding," wherein learning takes place not from a top expert to a novice, but from someone intermediate in skills to someone slightly less advanced. In nomadic tribes of Africa, the primary teachers of 5-year-olds are 6- and 7-year-olds. The primary teachers of 12-year-olds are 13- and 14-year-olds, and so on.

A related finding that Gray has uncovered pertains to the fact that all prewesternized societies have mixed-age learning as the norm. In his analysis, there are no examples of prewesternized societies in which age homogeneity typifies daily living conditions. That is, you don't tend to see an entire group made up of 10-year-olds and a separate group of only 15-year-olds, and so forth. Such age segregation during childhood only exists in the evolutionarily unnatural schools that permeate the lands of westernized cultures.

The relationship between scaffolding and mixed-age learning should be clear. Scaffolding can really only take place in mixed-age learning environments. So the primary form of human education—which was likely typical for thousands of generations before the advent of agriculture—is pretty close to nonexistent in the halls of "modern" schools.

Alloparenting and Extended-Kin Networks

Renowned evolutionist Sarah Blaffer Hrdy (2009) has spent a great deal of time studying the nature of parenting in human and nonhuman primates. In her book *Mothers and Others*, she comes to an important revelation that speaks volumes about the nature of childhood from an evolutionary perspective. Like Volk and Atkinson (2008), along with Gray (2011), Hrdy uses an evolutionary approach to help understand the natural state of parenting and to provide thoughts on how modern ways of doing things may be at least somewhat out of step with our nature.

In most other primate species, parenting is largely the job of the mother. This is true of the lion's share of mammalian species, in fact (largely as a consequence of females having necessarily higher levels of parental investment compared to males). However, as is true in humans, many other primate offspring are altricial and benefit enormously from multiple adults helping with rearing. Interestingly, in nonhuman primates, such as vervet monkeys, the primary helpers in the process (in addition to mothers) are other female adults often, but not always, related—including aunts, grandmothers, and the like. This relatively broad form of child care, which extends beyond the work of the mother, is termed *alloparenting*.

In prewesternized human societies, we see the same exact pattern of parenting. We see alloparenting. Parenting is not a one-woman job. And it's only rarely a male job. It takes a village to raise a child, and in prewesternized societies (and likely in the EEA of humans), this village includes mostly or exclusively females—a large proportion of whom are blood relatives with the child (who, thus, have a "genetic interest" in the success of the child). This help from extended-kin networks in childrearing is, in fact, the natural state of things when it comes to our species.

Nuclear families isolated from kin are typical in modern human societies. This is particularly true in large countries like the United States, in which kin may live 3,000 miles apart from one another. This is yet another example of childhood that can be elucidated and examined from an evolutionary perspective.

PARENT/OFFSPRING CONFLICT

As we learned earlier in this chapter, Robert Trivers is a master of coming up with clear and powerful theories of behavior and social relationships based on evolution. We saw this with

Parental Investment Theory, described earlier in this chapter, and we'll see this again here with Trivers' (1974) theory of Parent/Offspring Conflict. As with Parental Investment Theory, Trivers' theory of Parent/Offspring Conflict is applicable across species, including humans.

The basic point of Trivers' theory of Parent/Offspring Conflict is that while parents and offspring share an enormous amount in the way of shared genetic interests (each offspring shares 50% of his or her genes with Mom and 50% with Dad), the interests are not fully aligned. This is simply because while an offspring is 50% related to each parent, that offspring is 100% related to him- or herself. And each parent is 100% related to himself or herself. So between parents and offspring, from a strictly genetic perspective, there are overlapping and nonoverlapping points of interest.

The classic case where Trivers has documented Parent/Offspring Conflict pertains to weaning. All mammals are breastfed early in life. There comes a point at which it's time to stop breastfeeding. But when is the optimal time for such weaning to take place? Well, it depends on your perspective. If you're a mother who has other offspring, or the potential to bear future offspring, weaning should take place relatively soon. If you're an offspring who is 100% related to yourself and only 50% related to your mother and only 50% related to any full siblings, then an optimal time for weaning may be later. From such a scenario, it is not too difficult to envision how conflict can emerge.

Parent–child relationships are riddled with such conflict, and Trivers' theory helps us understand why this is. Further, this theory helps shed light on the nature of sibling relationships, which you may know from experience are not always perfect. Again, an individual has a genetic interest in the success of his or her siblings, as they share 50% of genes with an individual. However, there is, again, the issue of nonoverlap. Getting a disproportionate amount of time and investment from parents relative to other siblings is, mathematically, in the interest of any and all individuals. Clearly, this analysis gives rise to an understanding of familial relations that helps us understand the true (or ultimate) factors that underlie conflict within families. Parents and offspring don't always get along. Siblings don't always get along. And, ultimately, this is why.

SEX-DIFFERENTIATED DEVELOPMENT AND YOUNG MALE SYNDROME

Males and females are anatomically different and they have distinct life histories as a function of simply being male or female. Females have few gametes—and all these gametes are valuable. They grow up on a trajectory toward optimizing their potential reproductive success. Based on Trivers' Parental Investment Theory, discussed earlier in this chapter, females tend to gravitate toward long-term mating strategies and slow life history strategies. They tend to form close-knit circles and focus on social networks—a fact that matches the alloparenting that Hrdy (2009) discusses. In most prewesternized societies, female–female aggression is rare and typical female tasks include child care along with gathering and preparing food. In many ways, the developmental psychology of females seems to prepare them for adulthood, taking these factors into account.

The male world is different. In prewesternized societies, men hunt. They wage war. They fight other males within their own clan. Males live shorter lives with higher mortality rates than females (this fact is true across the entire life span; Kruger & Nesse, 2007). Male gametes, sperm, are cheap, plentiful, and available until late in life. Compared to females, males show a pattern of a relatively fast life history strategy. Male psychological development during childhood seems to match these factors.

A clear instance of behavioral differences between males and females across childhood and into adulthood pertains to what Martin Daly and Margo Wilson (1985) called *young male syndrome.* This "syndrome" essentially suggests that it's risky and, at times, unhealthy, to be a young male relative to a young female. Recent research has shown that males are significantly more likely to have had one or more significant injuries early in life (Johnsen, Kruger, & Geher, under review) compared with females. This fact corresponds to the fact that the male-to-female mortality ratio spikes in adolescence and early adulthood. This is to say that at all points of the life cycle, males die more frequently than do females. This sex difference is exacerbated during the late teen and early adult years. And these are exactly the years when mate selection is prominent in the life cycle.

Patterns of deaths among young males further tell an evolutionary tale of sex differences in life history. They are likely to die in altercations with other young males or as a result of physically risky behaviors, such as motorcycle riding or rock climbing. Females are less likely than males to encounter injury or death during adolescence and young adulthood as a result of these kinds of factors.

The evolutionary approach provides a framework for understanding young male syndrome. When female parental investment in a species is high, females tend to be the relatively discriminating (choosy) sex. When one sex is relatively choosy in mate selection, the other sex is more likely to engage in *display activities*—activities that ultimately have the effect of attracting mates. In human males, many such display activities are physically involved and often include direct competition with other males (just go out to the most popular college bar in your neck of the woods on a Thursday night at 2:00 AM and you'll see what I mean!).

Why are boys different from girls? Why are young adult males different from young adult females? Why do some psychological and behavioral processes seem to fall across male/female lines? Evolutionary psychology, in general, and Parental Investment Theory, in particular, go a long way in shedding light on these age-old questions.

IMPLICATIONS FOR PARENTING

Parenting is a notoriously difficult task. Nearly every cliché about the process has at least a kernel of truth behind it. As I document in a recent article on the nature of parenting from an evolutionary perspective (Geher, 2011), evolutionary psychology has significant implications for the nature of this momentous life task. A summary of these ideas is included here.

First and foremost, from an evolutionary perspective, there is no single behavioral domain that is more significant to the nature of being human than parenting. Evolutionary psychologists often talk about the importance of mating—as it's the key domain that bears directly on reproductive success—and this is a fair point. However, parenting also bears directly on reproductive success and is just as complex and nuanced as mating. Recent research in the field of evolutionary psychology has focused on mating—much of my own work included (see Geher & Kaufman, 2013). This said, it is without question that parenting is at least as evolutionarily significant—and an evolutionary approach has enormous potential to help elucidate the nature of parenting. Accordingly, this should be a major research topic of future scholarship.

As you can see from this chapter, the evolutionary approach has implications for many facets of parenting. As a way to help scholars and students focus on specific aspects of parenting that can benefit from this approach, my article (Geher, 2011) focuses specifically on (a) the nature of ancestral human social structures, (b) cheater detection as a significant human adaptation, (c) the evolution of human emotional reactions and expressions of moral outrage, (d) an evolutionary approach to understanding the importance of reputation in social groups, and (e) the evolution of reparative altruism. These topics are discussed briefly below to help provide a sense of how evolutionary psychology can help us understand the nature of parenting.

The Nature of Ancestral Human Social Structures

For several reasons already discussed in this chapter, it is important to remind ourselves of natural human social structures. Our ancestors lived in small groups of approximately 150, comprised largely of kin and of individuals with long-standing ties to one's kin network (Dunbar, 1992). To see what child development is in terms of our evolved psychology, sometimes it's best to look outside of Western cultures to see how things happen in prewesternized societies, where social structures and group size match the human EEA. Based on the content of this chapter, we can see that this approach helps us understand the nature of education, the fact that education in natural settings is not distinct from work or play, and that it is not primarily implemented by adults. We've also seen what a true "it takes a village" approach means in terms of human evolutionary history. It does take a village, and we call this feature of social behavior alloparenting (Hrdy, 2009). In humans, for thousands of generations, alloparenting has taken the form of female groups helping raise children in a cooperative manner.

Further, the fact that our evolved psychology is shaped to match the EEA has implications for how we raise our children. Even if you raise a child in a large westernized city, you need to understand that the child and the folks that he or she will encounter in life have psychologies that match the EEA—not the interesting yet unnatural nature of your current environment. Consider the following mismatches between modern city living and the EEA—all of which have clear implications for raising a child:

- Our ancestors rarely encountered strangers outside their clan. In a modern city, you can encounter thousands of strangers daily.
- Our psychology was not designed to anticipate such a large number of strange conspecifics. Thus, things like "stranger anxiety" that we see with young children are actually quite natural.

● Under ancestral conditions, family was broadly construed—large groups of adults, usually mostly female and usually interrelated—worked together to help raise offspring. Many of us now live in nuclear families with extended kin living miles away.

Cheater Detection As A Significant Human Adaptation

In relatively small and stable ancestral groups, cheating was easily detected and was likely severely punished. In this context, *cheating* could take the form of stealing from others, not doing one's share of the work, and so forth. Some of the strongest research in evolutionary psychology has shown that a basic aspect of our psychology is the ability to detect cheaters in such social contexts (Cosmides & Tooby, 1992). In large cities, when surrounded by strangers, opportunities to cheat in social contexts are rampant and are evolutionarily unprecedented. We need to teach our children not based on what's possible in large, unnatural cities, but what's appropriate given the evolved psychologies of those around us—psychologies that are not matched for modern westernized environments but that are, rather, matched to the EEA.

The Evolution of Human Emotional Reactions and Expressions of Moral Outrage

Since Darwin's (1872) treatise on the emotions of humans and animals, research on the nature of emotion has shown that the human emotion system is clearly a product of evolution, leading to such findings as the fact that the ability to accurately detect emotional facial expressions across cultures is nearly perfect (Ekman & Friesen, 1968). People often express negative emotions, such as outrage and anger, in response to breaches of social norms. This expression of outrage seems to serve a function of keeping others in the group in line (see Kurzban, 2010).

Our children can benefit from understanding the nature of emotions, why they exist, and what function they serve. Fostering such an understanding can help our children develop important emotional and social skills that are crucial for getting along with others.

An Evolutionary Approach to Understanding the Importance of Reputation in Social Groups

Children raised in modern westernized contexts may have a hard time discriminating what's possible in modern situations versus what would have been deemed appropriate under ancestral conditions. In a large city, a child can throw chewed gum on the sidewalk without much cost. And I think this probably happens—at least in New York! Under ancestral conditions, engaging in such socially questionable behavior would not only be more likely to get noticed (remember, it's a small group), but it would be more likely to lead to punishment and deleterious effects on one's reputation. A kid who did the equivalent of throwing gum on the sidewalk in an ancestral clan risked adverse effects to his or her reputation. A kid who does this on the busy streets of Manhattan does not. We need to raise our children not for the busy streets of modern Manhattan, but for the small, tight-knit villages that typified the environments of our ancestors.

The Evolution of Reparative Altruism

A final point regarding how evolutionary psychology can relate to parenting pertains to the nature of reparative altruism (Trivers, 1985). In writing about the moral emotions, Trivers discusses emotions as designed to help individuals maintain harmonious relationships with others in their group. Several actions that coincide with these emotions, such as being grateful or apologetic, seem to be part of our psychology to help us navigate the complex social waters in which we find ourselves.

Reparative altruism is essentially apologizing, and in a species such as ours, where we evolved in small stable groups functioning as a unit, apologizing for transgressions to the group writ large, or to individuals within the group, likely serves a function of keeping one connected to the group. In a species such as ours, keeping connected to the group is critical.

As we'll see in a later chapter on the evolutionary psychology of religion, religion likely evolved to help instill these kinds of behavioral features within ancestral groups (see Wilson, 2007). However, as many of us know, we don't need religion to be moral creatures, but nonbelievers among us certainly can take lessons from the believers in our midst. All the moral emotions that are underscored in religion after religion (see Wilson & Sober, 2002) are extremely valuable, and teaching the importance of these emotions (including guilt, pride, being sorry, making amends, etc.) to our children can go a long way in helping them develop into moral animals who are important contributors to groups in which they will find themselves.

SUMMARY: EVOLUTION AND CHILD DEVELOPMENT REVISITED

Humans are a slowly developing ape, and the evolutionary perspective takes this strongly into account by examining the nature of child development in terms of basic evolutionary theories of humans. Trivers' (1972) theory of parental investment helps explain why human development and parenting are so intensive in an altricial (slowly developing) species such as ours. During development, the formation of social and familial bonds is crucial in helping children develop skills needed to succeed in human groups. On the other side of the coin, issues of parenting are importantly highlighted by the evolutionary perspective, which focuses strongly on how parenting includes a constellation of behaviors designed to help facilitate long-term reproductive success.

DISCUSSION/ESSAY EXERCISES

- Describe Volk and Atkinson's (2008) basic premise regarding infant mortality. In your answer, describe the basic patterns of data that these authors document, and explain how the data demonstrate a cross-cultural and cross-historical perspective. Finally, describe the implications of this research for the psychology of parenting (including, in particular, parental reactions to death and injury of children).

- Describe Gray's (2011) ideas on modern educational systems and evolutionary psychology. In your answer, address how education takes place under nonwesternized conditions. Also, be sure to address the idea of *scaffolding*. Finally, briefly describe implications of this work for modern educational contexts.

- Briefly describe Hrdy's (2009) work on parenting in prewesternized contexts. In your answer, address the concept of *alloparenting*, and briefly comment on how her work implies that there is a mismatch between ancestral parenting structures versus modern, westernized structures.

Courtship, Intersexual Selection, and Intrasexual Competition: The Hot Ape

KEY TERMS

- Courtship
- Display behaviors
- Evolutionary explanations of menopause
- Evolutionary psychology and physical attractiveness
- Female-specific mating strategies
- Heritability
- Intersexual selection
- Long-term mating
- Male-specific mating strategies
- Mental fitness indicators

- Personality traits in mate selection
- Short-term mating
- Universals in mate attraction

ere's a puzzle for you: Think about the connections among these different phenomena:

- Kissinger (1973) said that "power is the ultimate aphrodisiac," and this sentiment is still highly quoted decades later.
- The Miss Universe competition, which includes women rated as "most attractive" in nations across the world, includes women who, regardless of country of origin, consistently have hour-glass figures and youthful faces (Cunningham, 1986).
- Male poets in England who are rated as relatively good at their craft have more sex partners than do male poets who are less poetic (Nettle & Clegg, 2006).
- Men with symmetrical faces have armpit sweat that is rated as "more attractive" by women than men with less symmetrical faces (Gangestad & Thornhill, 1998).
- Postmenopausal women are consistently rated as less attractive than their fertile counterparts (Gallup & Frederick, 2010).

So here we've got an apparent hodgepodge. I am essentially asking, "What do political power, youthful facial features, good poetry, armpit sweat, and menopause have in common?" Before the evolutionary approach was applied to issues of human psychology, no connections could be made among these seemingly unrelated phenomena. In fact, in light of theoretical and empirical advances in evolutionary psychology, the connections are clearer than you might think. Short answer: They all pertain to factors that underlie attraction to potential mates. The long answer is, essentially, the remainder of this chapter!

The current chapter, along with the next two chapters, focuses on issues of human mating. Importantly, in the language of evolutionary psychology, *mating* is about much more than just sex. Mating includes the entire gamut of behaviors and psychological processes that bear directly on the creation of offspring. Thus, human mating includes issues of courtship, dating, pair bonding, extra-pair relations, sexuality, and, very importantly, love.

This chapter focuses on relatively early aspects of the human mating process—courtship, intersexual selection, and intrasexual competition. These are the processes that underlie how individuals connect with one another in the mating domain.

COURTSHIP AND INTERSEXUAL SELECTION

Mate selection is not random and factors upon which individuals focus in mate selection make sense from an evolutionary perspective. In fact, in all sexually reproducing species, mate choice is biased (or nonrandom), and individuals focus on certain qualities that they look for in potential mates—while they are repulsed by other qualities.

In many bird species, males and females show *sexual dimorphism*, or the tendency to have differences between males and females. These differences are typically framed in terms of differential morphologies, or bodily features. Male blue jays are bluer than their female counterparts, and they have special tufts atop their heads, which are lacking on females. A similar difference is found in cardinals, as well as in many other species of birds.

When we see sex differentiation in morphological features in a species, this is usually a sign that there has been *intersexual selection pressure* created by the mate-selection choices of one sex—leading to, across evolutionary time, specific features that come to typify the other sex. Female blue jays are attracted to males with relatively bright plumage and a relatively pronounced tuft. Across evolutionary time, this fact has come to the current reality of male blue jays having relatively deep color and relatively pronounced tufts.

Darwin was fascinated by this issue, having dedicated one of his most renowned books to the topic of sexual selection, *The Descent of Man, and Selection in Relation to Sex* (1871). Darwin's classic example of intersexual selection pertained to peafowl (with males being *peacocks* and females being *peahens*). Sexual dimorphism is very pronounced in peafowl—males have elaborate and bright plumage while females are relatively drab. "Why would males evolve to have such conspicuous plumage?" Darwin wondered. From a strict survival-based perspective, such plumage seems disastrous. The jungles of Asia, where peafowl naturally roam, are filled with predators—not least of which includes tigers. They're scary! Bright, conspicuous plumage is the opposite of camouflage. It has the capacity of drawing the attention of predators *and* slowing one down (due to large, extra bodily features) if a chase should happen. However, this plumage is species-typical all the same! Darwin eventually came to a landmark realization that is now a backbone of modern evolutionary theory. It's the basic idea of intersexual selection—if members of one sex tend to choose mates based on such-and-such criteria (for whatever reason), these criteria will come to shape the nature of the members of the other sex. Under ancestral conditions, peahens must have had a preference for peacocks with relatively bright plumage, and this tendency came to the reality we see today at zoos across the country—peacocks have larger and brighter tails than peahens.

A major question that emerges from Darwin's theory of intersexual selection pertains to the issue of why members of one sex would show such a strong preference for some quality in the other sex in the first place. It turns out that, not surprisingly, there usually is a reason. In the case of the peacock's tail, Hamilton and Zuk (1983) found that males with relatively bright tails (relative to other males) were less likely to be infected by various parasites. Similarly, they found that the degree of symmetry of the plumage also corresponded to being relatively free of parasites. As we'll see in more detail in a later section on fitness indicator theory, being relatively free of parasites is likely a sign that an individual animal has a strong immune system and a relatively strong genotype underlying it—a genotype that would be beneficial in offspring.

In any case, some form of courtship can be documented in nearly all sexually reproducing animals. Sometimes courtship is physical in nature (with animals simply having physical features that are attractive to potential mates) and sometimes courtship is behavioral in nature (such as is the case of the blue-footed booby of the Galapagos Islands, in which the males does a special courtship dance to attract a female—and based on the quality of the dance, a female will determine if she will mate with the male).

As we shall see in subsequent sections of this chapter, human attraction and mate selection include a combination of the physical and the behavioral.

MALE/FEMALE SIMILARITIES AND DIFFERENCES IN ATTRACTION

In a recent book on the topic of mating intelligence that I co-wrote (Geher & Kaufman, 2013), we have a subheading in one chapter titled *Men Are from Springfield, Women Are from Springfield*. This subheading is a play on John Grey's (1992) famous book *Men Are from Mars, Women Are from Venus*. Differences are easy to spot, and differences are, in many cases, more interesting than are similarities—in any domain.

This said, an important but often overlooked aspect of human mating psychology is the fact that men and women are actually extremely similar when it comes to mate choice—and this finding is well documented. As Li (2008) found, under many conditions, men and women place equal emphasis on the importance of looks, love, intelligence, and several other features.

In a now-classic study of mate preferences across the sexes and across 37 different cultures, Buss and his colleagues (1989) found that when asked to rate how important various characteristics are in selecting a mate, men and women, across cultures, rated *kindness* and *mutual love* as tops. As we'll see, there do end up being several important and well-documented sex differences in the mating domain as well—but to make sure we don't lose the forest for the trees, it's important to start with the fact that males and females generally are looking for the same thing!

This said, the same research by Buss et al. (1989) found several consistent differences in the characteristics desired by males and females in potential mates. Compared to males, females tended to prefer a mate who was older than oneself and who was relatively ambitious, intelligent, and well-educated. Buss interprets these findings regarding female preferences in terms of Parental Investment Theory (Trivers, 1972). Specifically, Buss points out the fact that for women, parental investment is necessarily high, and garnering help with raising a family, by having a partner who has access to resources and who is likely to stick around—and who is relatively high on the local status totem pole—is what's needed in a mate. Mates who are ambitious and well-educated are likely to have these qualities relative to other men. Women are attracted to power, success, and status, largely because our female ancestors who were attracted to these qualities were more likely than others to become our female ancestors.

Compared to women in Buss et al.'s (1989) research, men showed a strong preference for physical attractiveness. Buss also explains this finding in terms of evolutionarily based principles. In short, in our species, a female's reproductive window is finite—it starts after menarche and it extends until menopause. There are many theories regarding why menopause exists so clearly in our species, but not as much in other species (e.g., Dawkins, 1989). One well-known theory pertains to the *grandmother hypothesis*, which suggests that for women at a particular life stage, helping raise one's grandchildren (who each share 25% of genes with the woman) is evolutionarily more likely to lead to benefits in terms of reproductive success than trying to directly reproduce more. Based on this idea, it is evolutionarily adaptive for women to stop ovulating as a motivator to invest more in grandchildren at a certain point.

These ideas on the nature of menopause, interestingly, strongly relate to male preferences in mates. And they relate, importantly, to what we conceive of as *attractive*. While the details of the role of physical attractiveness in mating are covered in detail in a subsequent section in this chapter, it's worth noting here that there is an important theme underlying characteristics associated with female attractiveness—a theme that is related to the issue of menopause. In short, female attractiveness seems like a marker that a woman is premenopausal. Such qualities include thick, lustrous, and colorful hair, smooth skin, and full lips, among others (see Buss, 2003). These are all qualities that track age. Postmenopausal women tend to have thin and grey hair, wrinkled skin, and thin lips.

Our male ancestors didn't count their birthdays. They couldn't directly ask a woman her age and then surmise if she was likely in her fertile years. In fact, like many evolved psychological processes, mate preferences are largely unconscious—and they evolved largely because they were predictive of (or correlated with) outcomes associated with reproductive success. On average, men who had a preference for women with relatively youthful features were more likely to mate with such women. Such women were, on average, more likely to be able to conceive. And men with such preferences, therefore, were more likely than men with alternative preferences (e.g., men with a preference for women with wrinkled skin) to successfully reproduce. This is how the fact of menopause and the nature of human courtship are interrelated.

SHORT-TERM VERSUS LONG-TERM MATING

Sometimes people are interested in a potential mate for the long haul, and sometimes people may be looking for just a short-term fling. It turns out that there seem to be distinct long- versus short-term mating strategies—and sometimes what people want in a long-term mate can be quite different from what they want in a short-term mate. This idea relates to Gangestad and Simpson's (2000) notion of *strategic pluralism* in mating (along with Buss and Schmitt's [1993] theories on mating strategies), which suggests that a plurality of strategies are employed when it comes to mating—and that there are multiple routes to mating success. Sometimes individuals successfully reproduce by using short-term mating tactics, and sometimes individuals successfully reproduce by using long-term tactics.

In a basic sense, research suggests that males may be more likely to pursue short-term mating strategies while females may be more likely to pursue long-term strategies. This idea of sex differentiation in general mating strategies follows from the prior section, which addresses ways that men and women are different from one another in the mating domain.

Perhaps the clearest study on the topic of male/female differences in the tendency toward short- versus long-term mating is found in a now-classic article by Clark and Hatfield (1989). In this research, two relatively attractive undergraduate research assistants—one male, one female—were included. The task of the research assistants was simple—at least conceptually. These research assistants were asked to approach the next single member of the opposite sex walking by in the quad. Their task was determined based on a random-number-generating system with one of three options. A third of the time, they asked the person to go on a date. Another third of the time, they asked the person to go back to his or her apartment. The final third of participants were asked by the research assistant to have sex. Yeah, this last one must have been somewhat difficult!

The data from the study are clear, as found in Table 3.1. Compared with the other questions, the first question was relatively long-term oriented. From there, the questions delve deeper into the domain of short-term mating (toward the blatant question of, "Will you have sex with me?"). Further, it is clear that men and women showed significant differences in their responses to the questions that tapped short-term mating. Men were more likely

TABLE 3.1 **FINDINGS FROM CLARK AND HATFIELD'S (1989) STUDY ON MALE/FEMALE DIFFERENCES IN MATING TACTICS**

	Male Responses (Percent Who Said "Yes")	Female Responses (Percent Who Said "Yes")
Question asked:		
"Will you go on a date with me?"	50%	50%
"Will you go back to my apartment?"	69%	6%
"Will you have sex with me?"	75%	0%

to respond positively to requests for short-term mating than were women. These data capture the essence of basic sex differences in mating strategies.

Importantly, the issue of short- versus long-term mating extends beyond simple male/female differences. A great deal of research shows that there is much variability within the sexes when it comes to mating strategies, and there are many situational or ecological factors that play a role in determining mating strategies that people employ.

To some extent, we can think of male long-term versus male short-term mating strategies. In the terminology of Kruger, Fisher, and Jobling (2003), some men are *cads* (i.e., short-term mating strategists) and some are *dads* (long-term mating strategists). To some extent, these differences may actually be genetic, with some males holding a constellation of hypermasculine traits and a tendency toward short-term mating strategies (Gangestad & Simpson, 2000). Additionally, these differences are clearly linked to environmental factors—such as prevailing sex ratio in a local social context. When males are in short supply (such as is the case at many liberal arts colleges at the moment), they are more likely to utilize short-term mating strategies, partly because such strategies in this kind of environment are likely to be successful.

Females also show a plurality of mating strategies. While a general tendency of females is to pursue long-term mating opportunities (see Buss, 2003), there are some contexts in which women are somewhat likely to transition to a short-term mating mode. One such context seems to be having grown up in harsh and unpredictable conditions (Belsky, 1997). With such an upbringing, females are more likely to pursue a *fast* life history strategy—and such a strategy corresponds to short-term mating tactics. Thus, while there are some general tendencies in the mating domain for each sex, there are clearly specific long- and short-term mating strategies that can be employed by either sex depending on context.

THE ROLE OF PHYSICAL ATTRACTIVENESS

You might think that physical attractiveness matters in the mating domain—particularly in terms of mate selection—and you'd be correct (Gallup & Frederick, 2010). As alluded to in a prior section, physical attractiveness includes a constellation of markers of fertility in women, which makes sense in evolutionary terms given the fact of menopause.

In fact, the evolutionary psychology of physical attractiveness may well be the most straightforward way to see how evolution directly relates to human psychology. Females are only possibly fertile for about 35 years within their life spans. Preferences on the part of males to mate with females who are within this window would have clearly been strongly selected (as males with preferences for females outside this window would have bitten the evolutionary dust by trying to mate with females who were not, on average, capable of producing offspring).

Features of female attractiveness strongly map onto this reasoning. Female attractiveness includes smooth skin, full lips, lustrous hair, and large eyes—all signs of relative youth (see Buss, 2003). Further, female attractiveness is found in certain bodily features such as scent (see Gangestad & Thornhill, 1998), voice (Pipitone & Gallup, 2008), and, importantly, waist-to-hip ratio (Platek & Singh, 2010).

Waist-to-hip ratio (WHR) seems to be a particularly important marker of physical attractiveness. This may be seen as the degree to which women have an "hour-glass figure." This ratio is simply the measurement of one's waist divided by the measurement of his or her hips (in terms of circumference). For instance, if a woman's waist is 30 inches and her hips are 40 inches, her WHR would be 30/40 = .75. If her waist size is equal to her hip size (e.g., each is 30 inches), her WHR would be 1.0.

Research on the nature of WHR has found that women with approximately a .7 WHR are rated as most attractive—by both men and women. This ratio seems to be consistent across both time and culture (Singh & Singh, 2006).

This all leads to the question of why WHR is so important in determining attractiveness. From an evolutionary perspective, there are good reasons. For one, WHR, due to the differential distribution of body fat across the sexes, is strongly sex differentiated—and it's a basic cue that people use to reliably determine if someone is a male or a female (Singh & Singh, 2006). Next time you are walking and see a person off in the distance, notice how you automatically use this cue to make a judgment as to whether the person is male or female.

Additionally, WHR is strongly affected by puberty (post-pubescent females are more likely to have a lower WHR that prepubescent females), pregnancy (pregnant females are less likely to have a low WHR than nonpregnant females), and menopause (postmenopausal women are less likely to have a low WHR than premenopausal women). WHR is a reliable marker of fertility. For this reason, it is a basic aspect of ratings of female physical attractiveness.

The factors associated with male attractiveness similarly show an underlying evolutionary reasoning. While men with a WHR that is close to .9 seem to be rated as most attractive (see Singh & Singh, 2006), in men, the shoulder-to-waist ratio of approximately .6 is rated as most attractive. This ratio, which corresponds to a muscular, v-shaped frame, is predictive of physical strength (such as the strength of one's handgrip; Gallup & Frederick, 2010). Women who mated with relatively strong males under ancestral conditions reaped the evolutionary benefits of (a) having offspring who were likely to have these adaptive traits and (b) gaining protection from a relatively strong man.

Other signs of attractiveness in males include markers of high testosterone, such as a relatively pronounced jaw, some facial hair, a muscular body, and a relatively deep voice (Gallup & Frederick, 2010). High testosterone actually can compromise one's immune system. Thus, researchers on this topic argue that markers of high testosterone serve as something of an evolutionary handicap (Zahavi, 1975). The fact that one can be healthy in spite of relatively high testosterone indicates that there is something special about an individual. This individual may have "good genes," so to speak, and, thus, would be a good catch in terms of producing offspring.

A significant contextual factor that pertains to ratings of attractiveness is whether a woman is near the peak of her ovulatory cycle—with ovulating women showing a suite of reactions and judgments that differ from nonovulating women. These findings are included in more detail in the next chapter, related to the evolutionary psychology of sex.

ATTRACTIVE PERSONALITY TRAITS

But, as you well know by this point in your life, there's more to life than looks. Buss et al.'s (1989) research on mate preferences clearly shows that kindness and mutual love matter—at least at a conscious level—more so than looks.

In our species, behaviors are complex, and behaviors often map onto basic personality traits, such as the Big Five personality trait dimensions of extraversion (being outgoing), neuroticism (being relatively emotionally unstable), openness (being open to new experiences), agreeableness (being easy to get along with), and conscientiousness (being diligent; see Costa and McCrae, 1992). Each of these basic trait dimensions is on a continuum and tends to be normally distributed. That is, most people in a population score as near average on each dimension, while some people score "high" on each dimension and others score "low" on each dimension—so one person may be very high on extraversion while another may be very low.

In an evolutionary analysis of basic personality traits, Nettle and Clegg (2008) found that these traits vary in terms of important mating-relevant functions, and high scores versus low scores on each of these dimensions seem to have evolutionary costs and benefits (which, according to Nettle and Clegg, account for why these dimensions are consistently found as normally distributed across populations instead of all people just scoring at a particular level of each variable). For instance, extraversion is attractive. All things equal, extraversion seems to be rated as positive in a potential mate. Further, likely as a result, extraverts tend to have more sexual partners than do introverts (i.e., people who score low on the extraversion dimension). You might ask, then, why all people aren't extraverts. Based on natural-selection reasoning, if extraversion is attractive and extraverts are more likely to turn up mating opportunities compared to introverts, shouldn't there be positive selection for extraversion across generations, wiping introversion out of the gene pool?

Well, it's not that simple. In their analysis of this issue, Nettle and Clegg (2008) found evidence that extraverts are more likely to be risk takers, are more likely to incur injury, and are more likely to die young. Well these are clearly evolutionary costs—costs that are not incurred by introverts at the same levels.

In short, Nettle and Clegg (2008) argue that each of the Big 5 personality trait dimensions has a relatively "attractive" pole, but there are always costs associated with scoring as extremely high on each dimension. Generally, they find that high extraversion, low neuroticism, high openness, high agreeableness, and high conscientiousness are relatively attractive. Again, while these are attractive, via a process called *balancing selection* (similar to the idea of evolutionary trade-offs), they also have costs.

ATTRACTIVE BEHAVIORS AND MENTAL FITNESS INDICATOR THEORY

Here's a puzzle—how does writing good poetry help you survive? And how would this skill have helped our ancestors survive on the plains of Africa during the environment of evolutionary adaptedness (EEA)? What about being a good dancer? Or an all-star pianist? Or a really great comedian?

Answer: These qualities would hardly help you out if you were surrounded by saber-toothed tigers.

So why did these qualities evolve? Why do human beings have such high levels of creativity in so many domains? Why are so many forms of art culturally universal? From a survival standpoint, we can understand why weapons exist, but why do humans spend countless hours decorating their weapons (Miller, 2000)? Time spent decorating weapons is clearly time that could be spent making new weapons.

A fascinating theory that addresses the issue of the evolution of human creativity was put forth by Geoffrey Miller (2000). This theory suggests that such complex human behaviors evolved not for survival-based purposes, but for courtship-related purposes. Being a great dancer doesn't help with fending off predators, but it may well attract members of the opposite sex (think Gangnam style!).

Like the renowned peacock's tail, according to Miller, markers of human creativity evolved not to facilitate survival but, rather, to facilitate courtship—to attract mates. As is the case with the peacock's tail, we need to think about why high-quality creative displays would be attractive in the first place—how would mating with individuals with such-and-such qualities facilitate one's own reproductive success? In other words, how and why would this kind of preference be evolvable?

Miller's explanation of complex human behaviors, known as his *mental fitness indicator theory*, rests on the following premises:

1. Due to consistent kinds of errors in the DNA replication process, some number of genetic mutations is inevitable.
2. The lion's share of genetic mutations have either neutral or harmful effects.
3. Mating with an individual with a high number of genetic mutations, thus, puts one's genetic lineage at risk.
4. The brain and nervous system, the most complex physiological system in the human body, are shaped by more than 50% of coding DNA.
5. Behavior, the observable outcome associated with the nervous system, is, thus, a window into a large proportion of one's DNA.
6. Assessments of the behavioral patterns of potential mates provide a window into one's genome—and, importantly, into a mate's number of genetic mutations (or *mutation load*).
7. We have evolved complex behaviors as they serve as fitness indicators. Showing effectiveness at displaying complex behaviors is, at the end of the day, attractive.

This theory provides a large-scale framework for understanding so many uniquely human and clearly nonsurvival-based aspects of humans—all from an evolutionary perspective. It may well help us understand the ultimate evolutionary reasons for so many complex behaviors that typify our species.

As further theoretical rationale for this theory, Miller (2000) points out several specific criteria that must be met for a trait to be considered as a fitness indicator. These criteria outline that a trait must:

1. Be observable to others.
2. Show large variability between individuals.

3. Have at least some heritable component.
4. Be hard to fake.
5. Exist in some manifestation across human cultures.

These criteria, which typify fitness indicators across the animal kingdom (such as the tail of the peacock), actually match so many classes of creative human behavior. Consider dancing. I don't know about you, but I simply don't have this skill. When I try to dance Gangnam style with my family, my kids laugh their heads off at me! "Dad, you can't do it!" I guess they're right! Let's think about dancing in terms of the different criteria for fitness indicators. Dancing is observable—nearly by definition. People may dance alone, but that's not typically the point. As mentioned earlier in this paragraph, there is strong individual variability in dancing ability. Sure, you can improve by taking classes, but to a large extent, you have it or you don't. Does dancing have a heritable component? I'm not sure if specific research on this exists, but to the extent that people seem to have it or not, it seems that there may well be a genetic substrate (research on behavior genetics usually finds some genetic basis to nearly all behavioral domains [Bouchard, 2007]). So is good dancing hard to fake? You bet—I couldn't fake it if I tried all day!

Clearly there are multiple domains of creative behavior—what one lacks in one domain (e.g., drawing) may be compensated for in another domain (e.g., sense of humor). This all said, Miller's theory of complex behaviors as having evolved primarily for courtship purposes definitely opens the door to a significant and new way of understanding issues of being human.

INTRASEXUAL COMPETITION

In the domain of attracting a mate, an important consideration pertains to outdoing the competition. Mate selection is something of a game, with all individuals trying to optimize their lot by ending up with the ideal mate. In such a scenario, competition exists in the form of what we call *intrasexual competition* (or *intrasexual selection*). The nature of intrasexual competition is somewhat sex specific, and in this section is presented separately for females and males.

Female/Female Competition

Fisher, Cox, and Gordon (2009) have clearly documented the fact that while females are much less likely than males to engage in physical altercations over mates, they compete over mates all the same.

In addition to using clothing and make-up to make themselves appear more attractive, females use various *rival-derogation tactics* in the process of trying to secure mates. Eliminating the competition is one way to bring oneself up. This is not a pretty aspect of human nature, but it seems to characterize much of who we are in any case.

Two primary ways that women derogate other women include (a) bringing down the reputation of other women or (b) derogating the physical appearance of other women (Fisher et al., 2009). In commenting on the reputation of another woman, a woman may refer to that other woman as promiscuous—and, as you may well know based on your understanding of the English lexicon, various words that are less flattering than "promiscuous" are often used. Further, Fisher's research has found that women derogate the looks of other women, commenting negatively on such things as skin complexion, weight, and body hair in efforts to bring down other women. Again, not pretty, but this happens.

Male/Male Competition

Compared to women, men are more likely to utilize a combination of verbal and physical tactics in derogating rivals within a mating context. Given how important status is for males in terms of attracting mates, it makes sense that males would attack the status of rivals in derogation efforts. And they do. Again, the lexicon tells a tale, with males using words such as loser, jerk, and lame-o (is that one still used?)—and worse—to bring down the reputation of competitors.

In addition to utilizing verbal derogation tactics, males often engage in physical altercations, with mating as a core issue. Such physical altercations might include fighting over access to women (see Wilson & Daly, 1985) or, as we'll see in more detail in a later chapter related to pair bonding, fighting other men who have been sexually active with one's mate.

As alluded to in the prior chapter on child development, male/male competition is often deadly—and it likely accounts for the steep increase in the male-to-female mortality ratio found in late adolescence and early adulthood—exactly when competition for mates is most intense (Kruger & Nesse, 2007).

SUMMARY: EARLY ELEMENTS OF HUMAN MATING

Human mating starts with nonrandom mate choice. Choosing a mate for a long-term mateship or for a long-term mating situation is an essential part of human social behavior from an evolutionary perspective, as mate choice bears on raising shared young and on important steps related to replicating one's genes across generations. In many ways, men and women show similar mating preferences—designed to find kind, loyal, and entertaining mates. Further, much in the way of mate selection is sex-differentiated, with men focusing more than women on markers of fertility and women focusing more than men on markers of access to resources and status. Miller's (2000) fitness indicator theory serves as a significant new theory of courtship, which focuses on ways that people display creative intelligence in unconscious efforts to attract high-quality mates.

DISCUSSION/ESSAY EXERCISES

- Gangestad and Simpson (2000) argue for the idea of strategic pluralism in human mating. What is this basic idea, and what does it imply regarding the characterization of evolutionary psychology as an immutable doctrine on human nature? What are some male- and female-specific mating adaptations that they describe, and how can these be understood from an evolutionary perspective?

- Describe parental investment theory as it pertains to understanding reproductive systems that characterize particular species, as well as how this theory helps us understand sex-differentiated mating strategies within species.

- Describe features of female-specific mating strategies in humans and address how David Buss explains these strategies in terms of parental investment theory. Also, describe several specific research findings that support this evolutionary perspective on female mating.

- Describe features of male-specific mating strategies in humans and address how David Buss explains these strategies in terms of parental investment theory. Also, describe several specific research findings that support this evolutionary perspective on male mating.

- Describe the basic ideas of Geoffrey Miller's (2000) theory of mental fitness indicators. In your answer, address the importance of traits that are (a) partly heritable, (b) conspicuously observable, (c) highly variable across individuals, (d) without clear survival value, and (e) manifest across cultures. Be sure to address the role that sexual selection is posited to have in shaping these traits.

Sex: The Excitable Ape

KEY TERMS

- Nonreproductively oriented acts of sexuality
- The evolutionary function of kissing
- Nonvaginal forms of sex from an evolutionary perspective
- Evolutionary theories of homosexuality and bisexuality
- Human genital morphology
- Sperm competition
- Ovulation effects on female behavior
- Ovulation effects on male behavior
- Evolutionary psychological implications for hormonal contraception
- Sexual coercion from an evolutionary perspective

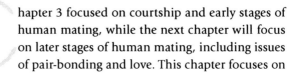 hapter 3 focused on courtship and early stages of human mating, while the next chapter will focus on later stages of human mating, including issues of pair-bonding and love. This chapter focuses on

what takes place in the middle—issues of sexuality from the perspective of evolutionary psychology.

As sex is the specific act that bears directly on reproduction, it makes sense that this is an important feature of evolutionary psychology. In fact, this has been a prominent topic in the field.

KISSING, FOREPLAY, AND NON-OBVIOUS REPRODUCTIVE SEX ACTS

As outlined in Chapter 3, human courtship is complex—including such varied acts as singing, dancing, conversations, joking around, flaunting looks, flaunting status, flaunting resources, and flaunting "good genes" by displaying high levels of creativity in public. Clearly, members of our species do a lot to get the attention of potential mates and to convince potential mates of our value. Often, courtship is extended—which makes sense in a species with high parental investment, such as ours.

Human sexuality includes a variety of acts that are essentially not obviously reproductive in nature. Mutual grooming and fondling (Nelson & Geher, 2007), kissing (Hughes, Harrison, & Gallup, 2007), and nonvaginal sex acts (Peterson & Geher, 2011) all speak to the extension of our complex courtship processes into the physical acts associated with sex itself.

In a large-scale study of the nature of human kissing, Hughes et al. (2007) asked over 1,000 young male and female adults a battery of questions regarding the nature of kissing. The results were revealing. Both males and females reported a strong focus on kissing as a mate assessment device. Participants reported the importance of a lot of kissing early on in a relationship. Females seemed to see kissing as a test of a male's commitment, which stems from the fact that females often test males' commitment as a way to find males who are relatively faithful and long-term oriented. Males, relative to females, showed a preference for "more tongue" and more overall salivary exchange (i.e., "deep kissing").

This fact may well pertain to a general tendency for males to unconsciously try to assess if a female is near her ovulatory peak—which makes sense from an evolutionary perspective, as females can only effectively conceive near an ovulation.

These researchers also found a difference when it comes to the importance of kissing. Overall, females rated kissing as more important than males did, across the board. Further, an interesting interaction emerged when participants were asked how important kissing is early on versus relatively later in an intimate relationship. Females rated kissing as more important than males at both times. Interestingly, however, for females, the importance of kissing increased when thinking about its role later in a relationship; for males, the effect of time was reversed. Males rated kissing as less important later relative to earlier in a relationship. This fact seems to mirror research on general sex differences in mating strategies. It seems that in thinking about kissing across the duration of a relationship, females see kissing largely about helping foster and maintain a relationship more than men do.

Various acts such as holding hands, hugging, and mutual grooming also seem to be important physical acts that serve as a bridge between courtship and sex (see Nelson & Geher, 2007). As is true of several species, including other kinds of primates, humans engage in a great deal of mutual grooming—stroking hands through one's hair, stroking nonerogenous parts of another's body, and so on. The nature of such grooming is not random. You're probably less likely to stroke the hair of the cashier at the checkout counter than the hair of your significant other, child, or close friend. Mutual grooming in our species likely started as a mechanism of parasite removal, but based on its role in romantic relationships (documented by Nelson & Geher, 2007), it has clearly become a bridge between courtship and more intimate acts.

Like kissing, grooming and other acts of foreplay provide an opportunity for individuals to (literally) feel potential mates out. If someone isn't a "good kisser," or is not comfortable with acts of grooming and other such intimate acts, this may be a signal that this person would not be a great mate—failing to show unconsciously accessible signs of commitment and secure attachment.

Peterson and Geher (2011) conducted a study examining the evolutionary psychology of various sex acts and found that adults clearly show variability in their preferences for different sex acts. Importantly, most of the acts described in this study were of the nonvaginal-intercourse variety. This fact is interesting from an evolutionary perspective as, clearly (hopefully you know this!), only vaginal intercourse leads to reproduction; oral and anal intercourse do not. Yet many participants in our research showed strong preferences for these kinds of acts.

One important question that emerges from this research is *why*? Why would nonreproductive-oriented sex acts be desired and come to be species-typical? Our research suggests that there are strong relationships between personality variables and preferences for particular sex acts, with extraverts and individuals high in sociosexuality (Simpson & Gangestad, 1991)—which is essentially promiscuity—corresponding to a preference for oral and anal intercourse (and, in fact, all forms of sex acts). There may be an overall sex-drive effect underlying these phenomena. Further, the research uncovered a clear sex-differentiated pattern, with females showing a much stronger preference for vaginal intercourse over other forms of intercourse, and males showing a stronger preference for all the different kinds of sex acts. Finally, there seemed to be an effect of mating intelligence (Geher & Kaufman, 2013), in which participants who scored higher on indices of the cognitive abilities that underlie mating tended to show a relative preference for vaginal intercourse.

In sum, human sexuality is complex, and its complexity matches the complex nature of human courtship. Various intimate acts that do not directly bear on reproduction are included in the suite of behaviors that are found in intimate relationships—with vaginal intercourse (the specific act that potentially leads to reproduction) being one of many such acts. Much of what we think of as sexual, in fact, seems to be largely about sizing up potential mates.

HOMOSEXUALITY AND BISEXUALITY

Speaking of sexual acts that do not directly bear on reproductive success, evolutionary psychologists are often asked about the evolutionary origins of homosexuality and bisexuality. If humans are organisms optimized to propagate their genes into the future, why would such nonreproductively oriented mating strategies come to exist at some level in cultures across the globe?

While this question is highly enigmatic and somewhat elusive within the landscape of evolutionary psychology, evolutionary psychologists have shed a good bit of light on this important facet of human nature. One theory that has received mixed empirical support pertains to the idea that homosexuals may be particularly prone to helping raise young kin (such as nieces and nephews). Based on this idea, homosexuality may emerge when resources are limited and an individual might benefit more in terms of long-term reproductive success by helping genetically related kin as opposed to reproducing him- or herself. Various other theories exist (such as the idea of male homosexuality being an attempt to join a male coalition [see Muscarella, 2000, for a summary])—and this is clearly an area of inquiry that warrants future research and examination.

This said, one thing that seems clear is the fact that homosexuality seems to differ markedly across the sexes (Hughes, Harrison, & Gallup, 2004). Males who are homosexual are more likely than females to be exclusively homosexual while female homosexuals (and heterosexuals) are more likely than males to report bisexual tendencies. In fact, research on the psychology of group sex suggests that male heterosexuals describe optimal group sex as including no other males, while female heterosexuals, when asked to describe optimal group sex, report an equal interest in extra partners being male or female. This finding, which speaks largely to female sexual fluidity, may result from a relatively polygynous history of our species, in which only males who held harems were part of the mating game—and that included multiple females. For a male, a situation with multiple male partners could lead to a conception that is not his, but a situation with multiple female partners, on the other hand, could lead to multiple conceptions that were all his. On the other hand, for a female, being included in such a harem would actually have been a positive outcome, being chosen to mate with the alpha male in a local ecosystem. Such a scenario may have included multiple females involved in sexual activities. This account is clearly speculative and implications would need to be tested empirically, but it is consistent with the findings of Hughes et al. (2004) on sex differences in response to factors surrounding group sex.

SPERM COMPETITION AND GENITAL MORPHOLOGY

In an eye-opening set of studies on human sexuality from an evolutionary perspective, Gallup, Burch, Zappieri, Parvez, Stockwell, and Davis (2003) examined the evolutionary function of the shape of a human erection. Trained as a primatologist, Gallup started this research with a question rooted in the issue of *sperm competition*, which is essentially the fact that males across many species seem to compete with one another to inseminate females, and various adaptations related to sperm competition have evolved. Gallup was particularly interested in human/chimpanzee differences. Relative to their body size, chimpanzees have much larger testicles than humans—and this fact is clearly related to an adaptation for sperm competition. Larger testicles create more sperm, and a relatively large blast of sperm makes it so that there is a higher chance of having one's own sperm (compared with the sperm of competing males) lead to conception within a female's vaginal tract. Such a morphological mechanism makes clear sense from an evolutionary perspective.

Humans may have relatively small testicles relative to chimps, but they also have more intricate erections. A chimpanzee's erection is without texture compared to a human's. A human erection includes the coronal ridge (which corresponds to the edge at the "head" of the penis) and the frenulum (which serves as something of a keel at the bottom of the erect penis). Perhaps, Gallup speculated, the shape of the human erection serves a role in sperm competition. So while chimpanzee males may have their large testicles for this function, human males have their evolutionarily engineered erections. Specifically, Gallup hypothesized that the details of the human erection serve a semen-displacement function. That is, the human erection is designed to remove sperm from competing males that may have been left in a female's vaginal tract from a prior copulation.

To test this theory, Gallup and his team had multiple artificial phalluses, some anatomically correct and some smooth like that of a chimp, inserted into an artificial vagina that was filled with a fluid designed to replicate the qualities of human semen. Simply, the researchers documented how much fluid was removed by each phallus. The data were clear—the anatomically correct phallus removed over 90% of fluid while the chimp-like phallus removed less than 30%. Like other details of human body morphology, the human penis seems to be shaped, literally, as a function of evolutionary processes.

In a follow-up study, the research team asked a group of sexually active male and female adults to describe the nature of recent instances of vaginal intercourse. Of interest, the researchers asked participants to describe the "strength" and "depth" of thrusting by the male as a function of whether the male thought that the female had been with another man recently. Consistent with the sperm-competition hypothesis, both males and females reported more and deeper thrusting when there was a suspicion of the female having had sex with another man.

THE EFFECTS OF OVULATORY CYCLE ON HUMAN BEHAVIOR

In 2007, Miller, Tybur, and Jordan published a highly publicized article relating to the nature of human ovulation and its effects on behavior. As recently as a few decades ago, scholars of human behavior considered humans as having concealed ovulation. That is, our species was considered to have females who ovulate in a discreet and unobservable way. In other primates, such as chimpanzees, to our senses, ovulation is quite conspicuous. During ovulation, female chimpanzees demonstrate intense genital swelling and a distinct and strong scent that signals males to her state.

Many scholars were interested in why human females do not show such conspicuous markers of ovulation. In fact, several theories of why ovulation is concealed in humans emerged (such as the theory that nonobservable ovulation allows women to confuse men as to who is the real father of a baby, perhaps obtaining parental investment from multiple males; Buss, 2003).

Recent research, such as that by Miller et al. (2007), actually paints a very different picture regarding the nature of human ovulation and its role in human social and sexual behaviors. Miller et al.'s work examined a very straightforward (if controversial) research question. Specifically, these researchers addressed if women who dance at strip clubs make more tips when they are near the peak of their ovulatory cycle (which corresponds to the body releasing high levels of the hormone estradiol) compared to when women are at other points of their cycle. One important factor that these researchers took into account was whether the women were currently taking hormonal contraceptives. Given the facts that hormonal contraceptives (a) are evolutionarily unnatural (that is, such contraceptives did not exist in the environment of evolutionary adaptedness [EEA]) and (b) that they trick a woman's body into a mimicked state of pregnancy, it made sense to examine their data separately from the naturally cycling women in the study.

Several findings emerged. When taken together, these findings tell a story of human ovulation not only being observable, but also as being significant in shaping important social and perhaps even economic outcomes. The dependent variable in this study was straightforward—the amount of money that women made in tips each day. In addition to measuring the amount of tip money, the researchers had women log into a computer to report how many days had passed since their last period to get a sense of where the women were in their ovulatory cycles. Tip earnings were approximately double during peak ovulation compared to other parts of the cycle for these naturally ovulating women, suggesting that somehow or another, ovulatory status affects behavior.

Interestingly, these effects were dramatically reduced for women taking hormonal contraception, suggesting that there may be important behavioral differences between women on hormonal contraceptives compared to other women (this point is addressed in more detail in the next section).

So what's going on? How do women who are near peak ovulation specifically behave differently from women at other parts of their cycle? And why?

As is typical of work in evolutionary psychology, it is useful to break these questions into *proximate* versus *ultimate* categories. Recall that proximate causes of behavior are immediate, specific factors that shape some outcome, while ultimate causes are the "big" causes of behavior, speaking to why some behavior or pattern was selected by evolutionary forces in the first place. Further, the work by Miller et al. (2007) speaks to the distinction between emitting signals (which is done by ovulating females) and detecting signals (which seems to be done by males—and perhaps other females) in regard to ovulation. If female strippers receive significantly larger tips when ovulating, then they must be emitting some kinds of signals—and men must be detecting these signals. So, interestingly, ovulatory effects seem to have important implications for the behaviors of both men and women.

In terms of proximate factors, hormonal estradiol levels, which do not fluctuate the same in naturally versus non-naturally (hormonal-contraceptive–using) cycling women, clearly play an important role in shaping signals of ovulation. The prevalence of this hormone in the body seems to prepare a woman for several outcomes. In fact, many specific bodily and behavioral changes have been documented in ovulating women. According to research findings reviewed extensively by Gangestad, Thornhill, and Garver-Apgar (2005) and Geher and Kaufman (2013), changes in female behavior and physiology that result from ovulation include:

- More female-initiated sex with partners
- A relatively strong preference for traditionally masculine partners (and a preference for features that indicate a good marriage partner as they move away from their high-fertility window)
- A higher likelihood of sexual infidelity
- A tendency to be more likely to touch males in casual social situations
- A tendency to be attracted to the scent of relatively symmetrical males
- A tendency to be attracted to relatively creative males
- A tendency to take more risks
- A tendency to be interested in erotic movies
- A tendency to wear relatively skimpy clothing
- A tendency to dance relatively dynamically
- A tendency for different body parts, including breasts, to be more symmetrical, among others (Geher & Kaufman, 2013, pp. 116–117)

Further, a great deal of research has found that ovulatory effects impact male psychology dramatically as well. In a review of literature on this topic, Geher and Kaufman (2013, p. 117) specifically describe the following:

SEX: THE EXCITABLE APE

- Males give bigger tips to female strippers who are ovulating
- Males find the voices of ovulating females relatively attractive
- Males find the scent of ovulating females relatively attractive
- Males report finding ovulating females physically attractive compared to photos of the same women when not ovulating, and more

In light of all this research, it seems that books on female sexuality need to be rewritten—we are not the "concealed ovulatory ape." Ovulation simply seems to be signaled by qualities that are relatively low on the radar when it comes to conscious processing.

All these features of ovulatory status bear on proximate factors that underlie our ability to detect ovulation. But this all begs the question of ultimate causation. Who benefits from ovulation in human females being able to be detected? How and why did these ovulation-signaling mechanisms evolve in our species in the first place?

Like many questions of ultimate causality, this one requires a bit of speculation. We don't know the answer in full. One possibility is that in a group of ancestral women who were constantly surrounded by one another, there was selection to catch up with other women in terms of ovulation. This would be particularly useful in polygynous, or harem-based systems in which one dominant male had access to multiple females. If one woman was ovulating, there would be pressure on the others to ovulate as well, to not "miss the boat" so to speak. And being able to effectively signal this status would also make sense from this perspective.

Clearly, more work on the ultimate causes of ovulation display and detection needs to be conducted. This said, it's noteworthy that the sheer amount of research on this topic has been extraordinary, and we can safely say that ovulatory status in humans has a significant impact on the psychologies of both women and men.

IMPLICATIONS REGARDING HORMONAL CONTRACEPTION

Looking back at Miller et al.'s (2007) research, it's noteworthy that women who were taking oral contraceptives were essentially excluded from the analyses, as their behavior didn't match the outcomes of the naturally cycling women. Statistically speaking, this is fair enough. But if you think about the implications of this for modern society, there's reason for pause. The number of women who take hormonal contraceptives in modern societies is very large. These women do not ovulate. Several studies have shown that they do not show the same behavioral patterns as found in naturally cycling women.

A later chapter deals with implications for evolutionary psychology on broader issues of society—but, for just a second, think about the implications of hormonal contraception on modern society. A large proportion of women, women taking hormonal contraceptives, are less likely to experience all the features already described regarding peak ovulation of naturally cycling women. They may dance less at parties, show less explicit interest in sex with their partners, and be less likely to engage in infidelity, for example. Note that, importantly, this is not a judgment call right here—just some provocative thoughts on societal implications of hormonal contraception (thoughts that are unearthed by research in the field of evolutionary psychology).

SEXUAL COERCION

Sexual coercion is clearly a significant and difficult social problem. In a recent book that I coauthored with Scott Barry Kaufman (2013, pp. 118–119), we examine this issue in detail from an evolutionary perspective, as follows:

Is sexual coercion an evolved mating strategy? This question may well be one of the most controversial questions in all of evolutionary psychology. The issues involved ultimately get to the issue of whether rape is an adaptation—and, if so, if there is something natural about rape. You don't have to think too hard to see how contentious this topic is. Right off the bat, we want to note that no research, no matter what it shows, should condone rape.

With this important point out of the way, there has been some research on this front. In a provocative book on this topic, *A Natural History of Rape: Biological Bases of Sexual Coercion*, Craig Palmer and Randy Thornhill argue that rape is part of a conditional mating strategy—utilized as something of a last resort after alternative strategies fail. Male scorpionflies try to obtain mates by one of three strategies. First, they try to carve out a nice territory on a fresh carcass ("Look, my pad's got a water view and it's near town!"). If that doesn't work, they dance in front of the females—showing off their symmetrical bodies. Well, this second strategy really only works if they have symmetrical bodies! A final (and least successful) strategy is used as a last resort—and it is essentially forced copulation.

Are humans like scorpionflies? Do males resort to forms of sexual coercion as a result of the failure of other mating strategies? Is, then, sexual coercion a form of a mating strategy?

On this point, there are a few broad schools of thought within the evolutionary literature. The idea of forms of sexual coercion as an adaptation has been studied extensively—with very interesting data sets that speak to this idea.

Importantly, all mating occurs in a social context, including a broader community. Wilson and colleagues argue that if we're thinking about rape from an evolutionary perspective, we should focus on how such an act affects the whole community. If there's a known rapist in the community, this adversely affects everyone. Being a rapist is not so great for one's reputation. Although a single act of rape may have fitness-enhancing consequences in the short-term, it is likely to have severely negative consequences in the medium- and long-term.

Being beaten up or killed by the male kin of a rape victim is not very good for passing on genes. Getting labeled as a rapist in a small community is extremely detrimental for developing strong alliances and social networks. The long-term fitness consequences of acts of sexual coercion are dramatic and negative within most human communities.

THE BROADER CONTEXT OF SEXUALITY WITHIN EVOLUTIONARY PSYCHOLOGY

Given the central role of reproduction within an evolutionary framework, it makes sense that evolutionary psychologists have studied a great deal of phenomena regarding human sexuality. As this chapter indicates, evolutionary psychologists have studied such facets of sexuality as foreplay, kissing, grooming, variety in sexual positions, sperm competition, sexuality across the ovulation cycle, sexual coercive behaviors, and more.

In the next chapter, we'll delve into the construct of mating intelligence (Geher & Miller, 2008), which speaks to the cognitive processes that underlie issues of human mating. As a precursor, it's useful to mention mating intelligence here, as it serves as something of a conceptual bridge between sexuality and broader issues of mating. Mating intelligence partly relates to issues of sexuality (such as the ability to know if a partner has been sexually faithful), but it largely deals with issues of mating that expand beyond the boundaries of sexuality, including such phenomena as the ability to attract mates with acts of kindness. The point here is this: Sexuality is really a slice of mating—and mating is a really a slice of the broader set of human behaviors that are social in nature.

So in the lexicon of evolutionary psychology, "mating" encapsulates much more than just sexuality. It includes how we court mates, how we form alliances, how relationships stay positive, and how mateships serve an important function in childrearing. The next chapter deals with the pair-bonding element of mating—with a focus on how evolution has turned us into the pair-bonding ape!

SUMMARY: SEXUALITY IS NO SMALL EVOLUTIONARY DETAIL

Sexual behaviors are central to human evolution, comprising the specific acts that lead to reproduction of genes into future generations. In humans, sexuality is complex, including many acts that are not directly related to reproduction, such as kissing and other acts of foreplay. Further, the nature of human sexual psychology and morphology, such as the shape of the human erection, can be strongly elucidated from applying an evolutionary lens. This perspective helps us understand such disparate phenomena as sexual orientation, the variety of sexual acts in humans, the effects of ovulation on behavior, and the nature of coercive sex acts.

DISCUSSION/ESSAY EXERCISES

- Briefly describe Gallup et al.'s (2003) idea of the human penis—a semen-displacement mechanism. In your answer, address how the findings from this research explicate the "selfish gene" view of evolution.
- Miller et al.'s (2007) research argues against the idea of "concealed ovulation." What evidence do they present to argue against this idea? How does nonconcealed ovulation make sense from an evolutionary perspective?
- Ovulation has been found to have effects on both male and female behaviors. Briefly describe at least two examples of each of these kinds of effects (two for males and two for

females). Finally, briefly describe how these effects have been explained from an evolutionary perspective.

- Briefly describe perspectives on sexual coercion that relate to evolutionary psychology. In your answer, address how Wilson et al. (2003) discuss this topic and how they conceptualize sexual coercion in a broader social context from an evolutionary perspective.

Pair-Bonding: The Somewhat-Monogamous Ape

KEY TERMS

- Pair-bonding
- Monogamy, polygyny, and polyandry
- Love from an evolutionary perspective
- Sex differences in infidelity
- The importance of "interloper proximity" in reactions to infidelity
- Physiological reactions to infidelity
- Cuckoldry
- Paternal-assurance tactics
- Semen chemistry from an evolutionary perspective
- *Mating success* versus *reproductive success*

- *Courtship display* components of mating intelligence
- *Mating mechanism* components of mating intelligence
- Facets of mating intelligence

et's start with a series of questions. What is love? Why do people fall in love? Why do people fall out of love? Why does divorce exist? Why does monogamy exist in some cultures but not others? Are humans truly monogamous?

These questions, which all bear on issues of long-term mating, speak to the fact that, unlike most mammals, humans often form long-term partnerships in the mating process. As do emperor penguins. As do many other kinds of species. Going back to Trivers' (1972) theory of parental investment, we can clearly see a linkage between altricial (slowly developing) offspring of a species and the nature of mating within that species. Long-term mating only evolves in relatively altricial species—species that, in other words, take a good bit of time to develop and have young who are relatively helpless early in life. Emperor penguins pair up for an entire breeding season. During this season, the couple cares for a single, large (and fragile) egg that houses a single chick inside. And if they succeed in this long and intense endeavor, they'll likely meet up again and enter a partnership during the next season.

Humans are a lot like emperor penguins as far as parental investment is concerned. Human females give birth to (typically) a single helpless baby that needs years and years of high-level attention to be able to survive. Having a father around to help clearly has adaptive benefits. As we've discussed earlier, this fact has shaped female psychology to focus largely on markers of a man being "long-term material" in the mate selection process. In this chapter, we explore other issues in human mating that pertain to long-term mating—or what we often call *pair-bonding*.

MATING SYSTEMS

Several kinds of mating systems exist across animal species. From short-term mating systems in many mammals such as beavers, in which mating consists of finding a mate, courting, and copulating, to long-term mating systems (typified by a pair staying together beyond courtship and often beyond a single breeding season) found in many species of songbirds, such as robins who dot our lawns in spring and summer. Within human cultures, multiple kinds of mating systems exist. We are familiar with monogamy in which one woman and one man pair up together exclusively. But other kinds of systems exist as well. In a very few cultures, polyandry (meaning multiple male partners with one female) exists. In such cultures, as in the Toda of India (Hughes, 1988), interestingly, the multiple males tend to be brothers—thus making it so that any shared young are genetically related to the different adult males in the group. More common is polygyny (meaning multiple female partners with one male). In polygynous societies, which are represented in cultures across continents (particularly in areas with high pathogen stress), it is typical for a dominant male to acquire multiple female partners in something of a harem-like system (see Low, 1990).

Thus, monogamy is not the only possible human mating system. But monogamy is common—and parental investment theory (Trivers, 1972) can help us understand why. For females, monogamy can be adaptive; if a female can secure a high-quality and faithful long-term partner, such an outcome would help in raising altricial offspring. And for males, monogamy can be adaptive really for the same reasons. A male who deserts a female after impregnating her risks the possibility of his offspring receiving insufficient care during development. So while a male may be better positioned to pursue multiple partners via a short-term mating strategy, being a solid long-term mating strategist and helping to foster a monogamous bond are clearly strategies that have the

91

potential to lead to reproductive success in males. Monogamy seems to have slightly different costs and benefits across the sexes, but it clearly does have conceptual reproductive benefits for each sex—a fact that helps explain the high prevalence of monogamous (or quasi-monogamous) mating systems in our species.

LOVE

Like many psychological processes that have been examined from an evolutionary perspective, love has been documented to have both proximate and ultimate causes. Love seems to be a universal human emotional state, tied to feeling deeply connected to another. Helen Fisher has conducted some very high-profile work on the physiology of love, demonstrating that feelings of love seem to correspond to the release of high levels of oxytocin in the brain, with a particular neurophysiological state seeming to characterize the experience of love.

Many other proximate factors seem to underlie love experiences, with members of couples who report being deeply in love experiencing relatively high levels of kissing (see Hughes, Harrison, & Gallup, 2008), mutual grooming (Nelson & Geher, 2007), and many other nondirectly-reproductive kinds of behaviors that seem to serve a proximate function of facilitating the connection of the pair-bond.

From an ultimate point of view, love clearly serves as a psychological experience that fosters pair-bonding—and this ultimately is rooted in the fact that we have altricial young. If human offspring were able to walk within a day of birth (e.g., such as white-tailed deer), our species would not benefit from biparental care, and monogamy would likely be nonexistent (as is the case in white-tailed deer). As we've seen time and time again in this book, proximate causes of behavior consistently map onto ultimate causes of behavior—this is how the relationship between evolution and behavior works.

INFIDELITY

While monogamy is common in many human societies, it is not universal. And in places where monogamy is normative (e.g., the United States), a high proportion of mateships dissolve for one reason or another in spite of this fact. For these reasons, it may be better to conceptualize humans as a *semi-monogamous* ape. Related to this point is the fact that infidelity is an important aspect of the human mating domain. *Extra-pair relationships*, or having sexual or emotional relationships outside of a pair-bond, comprise a significant aspect of mating.

In an eye-opening set of studies relating to the societal impact of infidelity, Daly, Wilson, and Weghorst (1982) examined homicide records from several large cities in North America—and what they found was striking. Over 25% of homicides had something to do with infidelity, including a male killing his partner who presumably cheated, or killing the interloper involved, or dying along the way in a confrontation along these lines. Infidelity is not a small detail when it comes to important social issues. In fact, such famous names as Bill Clinton, Eliot Spitzer, and John F. Kennedy all come with tales of infidelity that will permanently live in the ethos of our culture.

Much research has been conducted to address the question of what comprises infidelity and what factors predict the different reactions to infidelity. Theoretically, infidelity can be seen as a threat to one's reproductive success—particularly with a species with pair-bonding–related mating systems. If your partner cheats on you, that may lead to the partner (a) leaving you and your offspring and/or (b) having biological offspring with someone else. Either of these outcomes alone can be evolutionarily taxing. The combination of them would clearly be particularly detrimental to your long-term reproductive success.

Given how evolutionarily significant the costs of infidelity can be, it makes good sense that our psychology would be shaped to help us detect and inhibit infidelity. And this is exactly what we tend to find (see Buss & Haselton, 2005). Infidelity is a major cause of relationship distress and dissolution (see Fisher et al., 2009) and, as we have seen, it can lead to physically adverse outcomes such as homicide (Daly et al., 1982).

Some of the adaptations designed to preclude infidelity within a mateship are sex differentiated. That is, some of these adaptations play out differently for males than for females—and the patterns we observe seem to make sense in terms of evolutionarily based predictions. The best-known research on this topic comes from David Buss and his colleagues (Buss, Larsen, Westen, & Semmelroth, 1992), who first documented that men and women seem to react differently to prompts related to infidelity. Guided by an evolutionary perspective, these researchers theorized that the primary adaptive hurdle for women, when it comes to infidelity, is losing a partner's help, time, and access to resources. That is, if a primary mating goal of a woman is to find a faithful and high-quality male who has access to resources, having that partner cheat may signal a loss of all these features. For this reason, the researchers predicted that women (compared with men) would be particularly distressed about their partners cheating in an "emotional" sense—by falling in love with someone else. This prediction essentially sees such emotional cheating as a possible precursor to abandonment.

On the other hand, men have an adaptive hurdle regarding infidelity that women do not have. This particular adaptive hurdle pertains to the possibility of *cuckoldry*, or raising an offspring that is not one's own. Given the facts regarding reproduction and internal fertilization in our species, it's "Mama's baby" and "Papa's maybe." That is, with the exception of some very recent biotechnological advances, women can be certain that their baby is "theirs"—men cannot. In fact, a recent DNA-based analysis conducted across several countries around the world found that more than 10% of offspring tend to actually be sired from a father different than the man who thinks he is father (Anderson, 2006). Thus, this issue actually comprises a significant evolutionary hurdle. For this reason, Buss et al. (1992) argue, it would make sense that men would be particularly distressed by thoughts of sexual infidelity (i.e., their partner cheating by literally having sex with another man).

In a series of now-classic studies on this topic, Buss et al. (1992) found evidence for this predicted sex difference in reactions to infidelity. In one study, these researchers asked people to simply choose which situation would be more distressing of two options. The first option briefly described a situation in which the partner seems to be falling in love with someone else while the second option briefly described a situation in which the partner was having sexual relations with another. Simply, men were more likely than women to choose the "sexual infidelity" option while women were more likely than men to choose the "emotional infidelity" option. In an additional study, these researchers connected participants to electrodes to measure various indices of autonomic nervous system responses (such as heart rate) as a way to measure a nonconscious physiological stress index. Male and female participants were presented with thought samples of emotional infidelity and sexual infidelity. Men showed a stronger physiological response to the thoughts of sexual infidelity while women showed a stronger response to thoughts of emotional infidelity. And many studies since this classic article have supported this same general pattern.

In one follow-up study (Fisher et al., 2009), we asked participants to rate how distressed they would be in thinking that their partner cheated on them as a function of several variables. One variable pertained to the "proximity between the participant and the interloper." Four levels of "interloper" were used, including a stranger, a prostitute, a best friend, or a sibling of the participant's same sex. Interestingly, we found that participants reported more distress as the interloper got closer to the participant's inner circle. That is, people were most distressed thinking of the partner cheating with a sibling, followed by friend, prostitute, then stranger.

From a strict fitness-optimization perspective, we were a little surprised—having one's partner cheat with one's sibling would still increase one's representation in the future of the gene pool due to the overlap in genes shared with the sibling. What we found, however, was that the idea of one's partner cheating with a sibling was particularly distressing. We interpret these data in terms of the evolutionary significance of betrayal. In a species such as ours that lives in stable social groups, betrayal by one's sibling and romantic partner would be an extreme sign of a drop in status within one's social circle. In the long-term, people are sensitive to markers of such status changes—and this fact makes good sense as such status changes could have an enormous impact on one's ultimate long-term fitness. For this reason, we believe that infidelity with members of one's social or familial circle may well be the most devastating form of infidelity from an emotional perspective.

SPERM COMPETITION REVISITED (AND THE MANY FORMS OF PATERNAL-ASSURANCE TACTICS)

In the prior chapter, we discussed forms of sperm competition; that is, ways that males within a species compete with one another to impregnate females. Such competition may take many forms—from morphological/anatomical features such as the shape of the human erection (Gallup et al., 2003) to details of semen chemistry, such as a possible spermicidal element found in human seminal fluid (Gallup, Burch, & Berens Mitchell, 2006) likely designed to kill the sperm cells of rival males found in the female reproductive tract, to behavioral patterns, such as the killing of lion cubs sired by the prior alpha male by the new male once he takes over a harem. In each of these cases, there's an adaptation designed to have one's own sperm cells—and not the sperm cells of another male—fertilize the egg of a female.

Sperm competition may be seen as related to the broad area of paternal-assurance tactics. In his work on this topic,

Gordon Gallup (see Gallup et al., 2006) conceptualized paternal-assurance tactics existing at multiple stages regarding relationship development as shown in Table 5.1.

The physical and behavioral features described in Table 5.1 tell a story of human males having evolved to address the issue of paternal uncertainty in a multifaceted manner that includes behavioral, physical, and chemical means to try to reduce the likelihood of cuckoldry.

During the mate-selection phase of a relationship, males are particularly attracted to females who show strong signs of faithfulness—particularly in their search for long-term mates (Buss, 2003). During the courtship/dating phase early on in a relationship, males engage in a great deal of mate guarding (see Buss, 2003), taking steps to prevent other males from accessing

TABLE 5.1 **PATERNAL-ASSURANCE TACTICS ACROSS RELATIONSHIP STAGES**

Stage	Evolved Paternal-Assurance Tactic
Mate-Selection	Choosing female partners who show signs of faithfulness and fidelity for a long-term relationship.[1]
Courtship	Mate guarding—keeping one's mate away from potential rivals.[2]
During Sexual Activity	Physical adaptations such as a penis that acts to displace semen of competitors[3] and seminal fluid with spermicide to ameliorate sperm of competing males.[4]
Birth of Child	Checking to see that the offspring resembles the father.[5]
Across Relationship	Reacting angrily to signs of sexual infidelity.[6]

[1]Buss (1989).
[2]Schmitt (2004).
[3]Gallup et al. (2003).
[4]Gallup et al. (2006).
[5]Platek, Burch, Panyavin, Wasserman, & Gallup (2002).
[6]Buss et al. (1992).

their female partners. This often takes the form of a male being overly jealous and having concerns about his female partner "going out" without him. During sexual activity, several physiological adaptations seem to serve a paternal-assurance function. These include the semen-displacing nature of the male erection (Gallup et al., 2003) and the spermicide found in male seminal fluid that seems designed to destroy the sperm of rival males (Gallup et al., 2006). Paternal assurance is such a major issue in our evolutionary history that things don't end there. Once a child is born, there are clear efforts on behalf of the father and the father's family to assess resemblance between the new baby and the father (Platek et al., 2002). Further, across the entire relationship, male sexual jealousy seems like a significant emotional feature that serves a paternal-assurance function.

MATING SUCCESS

Darwin's bottom line is ultimately reproductive success. Whether some feature of an organism makes it into the future depends importantly on whether that feature facilitates reproductive success.

However, in research on humans from an evolutionary perspective, there is a problem with tapping Darwin's bottom line. In thinking about this problem, I think it's often useful to start by thinking about fruit flies. Fruit flies have a life span of about 2 weeks. Biologists love fruit flies largely for this reason. You can breed many generations of fruit flies in a short period of time and test things such as whether manipulations of one gene have positive or negative effects on the reproductive success of offspring. Also, importantly, fruit flies don't wear condoms—a point that actually comes into play in this discussion.

Now think for a minute about humans. For many reasons— some practical and some ethical—we can't do this same kind of research on humans. For one, people tend to live for about eight decades or so. You can't easily study 20 generations of humans within a 1-year laboratory experience. We're not like fruit flies in this way! Also, even if you could study many generations of humans in this manner, you couldn't! Think about the ethics of it. If you manipulated the genes of individuals before they became zygotes and controlled the experiment to differentially breed some humans and not others, you might not win the ethical-scientist-of-the-year award! And even if all of this were somehow surmountable, there's the issue of contraception.

In postcontraceptive societies, individuals who might have had extraordinary reproductive success might not reproduce at all due to the effective use of contraception. As such, practical and ethical issues aside, in a society like ours, the number of offspring is not necessarily a reliable marker of the kinds of adaptations that we associate with the evolutionary perspective. Darwin's bottom line is about the number of offspring produced into the long-term future (not total number of offspring, but number of offspring that succeed and make it to the future to reproduce viable and successful offspring). In a postcontraceptive society, we really can't measure reproductive success in this way.

As a consequence of these logistical and ethical issues, evolutionary psychologists have created measures of *mating success*. Mating success is essentially a proxy for reproductive success. It is not simply a measure of the number of times one has had sex or the number of partners that one has had, but it is a sex-differentiated measure of qualities that would have likely led to high reproductive success in the environment of evolutionary adaptedness (EEA) (see Geher, Camargo, & O'Rourke, 2008).

Mating success is conceptualized in a sex-differentiated manner, as the things that led to the reproductive success of our female ancestors were often quite different from those that led to the reproductive success of our male ancestors. For male ancestors, total number of sex partners was predictive of reproductive success; for our female ancestors, it probably was not. In other words, for females, more partners did not directly lead to the creation of more viable offspring. For females, one of the newest measures of mating success (see Geher et al., 2008) taps whether male partners have given much in the way of time and material resources. For males, this measure assesses how many physically attractive sex partners an individual has had.

The creation of psychometrically and behaviorally valid measures of mating success is still in the works. Work along this front has the potential to lead to the creation of proxies for Darwin's bottom line (reproductive success) that can be used to examine a broad array of hypothesized psychological adaptations.

MATING INTELLIGENCE

To this point, we've discussed a battery of psychological adaptations designed for mating-relevant purposes—from basic preferences in mates that relate to mate selection, to processes related to basic preferences regarding sexuality, to the psychology of infidelity. Without question, evolutionary psychology has shed extraordinary light on our understanding of mating.

In a recent set of books and articles designed to integrate these disparate aspects of mating psychology, I (along with several outstanding students and colleagues) have developed the construct of mating intelligence (Geher & Kaufman, 2013; Geher & Miller, 2008), which speaks to the entire set of cognitive processes that underlie human mating psychology. Mating intelligence includes cognitive processes that bear on such facets of human life as:

- Assessing one's own mate value
- Assessing the mate values of potential mates
- Displaying oneself in an attractive manner
- Using creativity effectively in mating contexts
- Effectively discriminating dishonest mating signals from honest signals (such as teasing apart someone who simply presents himself as high in status from someone who actually is)

● Effectively assessing the mating-relevant thoughts of potential and actual partners

Mating intelligence is a broad construct that we think ties together the many different facets of mating psychology. An important feature of mating intelligence is the fact that it includes both human universals as well as individual-difference–based aspects of human psychology. For instance, a basic aspect of human mating intelligence is the ability to know the qualities desired by potential mates. In one study on this topic (Geher, 2009), a large sample of men and women were presented with personal ads written by members of their own sex. In one phase of this study, people first read a sample of the ads written by members of the opposite sex and rated which ones they would prefer for either a short- or a long-term mating partner. In the second phase, people rated the ads written by members of their own sex and worked to guess which ones were rated by members of the opposite sex as attractive for short- and long-term mating. Interestingly, male and female judgments seemed optimized. Men were particularly good at guessing which ads women liked for a long-term mate, and women were particularly good at guessing which ads men liked for a short-term mate. So it seemed that the mating intelligence of one sex was optimized to assess the dominant mating strategy of the opposite sex.

These findings regarding general tendencies in assessing the desires of the opposite sex speak to an attempt to assess a human universal—a general trend in how people assess the desires of potential mates. That said, the findings don't speak directly to individual differences in this ability. In an effort to examine individual differences in the ability to read the minds of potential mates, a team of researchers (O'Brien et al., 2010) used a psychological test called the Mating Intelligence Scale (Geher & Kaufman, 2007) to measure individual differences in this reported ability. It turned out that scores on this measure were strongly predictive of mating-relevant outcomes such as the number of sexual partners one had in the past year (this relationship was particularly strong for males, which makes sense as a high number of sexual partners in a short amount of time matches an optimal male strategy more than an optimal female strategy).

In any case, these studies in combination speak to the fact that mating intelligence addresses both human universals in mating-relevant cognitive processes (such as general tendencies in the ability to read the desires of the opposite sex) and individual differences in these processes (with the idea that some people are simply better at this ability than are others).

Another basic aspect of mating intelligence pertains to the distinction between what we call *courtship display mechanisms* and *mating mechanisms* (Geher et al., 2008). As you may recall from the prior chapter on mate-selection processes, Miller (2000) developed a theory of human creativity based on the premise that creative processes, such as musical ability, evolved largely to serve as a mate-attraction function (based on the idea of creative abilities as fitness indicators). We refer to these processes as courtship display mechanisms of mating intelligence—important aspects of our psychology that serve a mating function, but that don't directly relate to mating-relevant issues. On the other hand, the *mating mechanisms* of mating intelligence include the cognitive processes that directly relate to issues of mating—such as assessing one's own value as a mate, modifying one's mating strategy as a function of ecological conditions, accurately detecting deception in the mating domain, and so forth. In combination, we refer to these processes as *the mind's reproductive system* (Geher & Miller, 2008).

In a unifying framework regarding mating intelligence, we see courtship display mechanisms and cognitive mating mechanisms as independently predicting mating success (our best approximation for Darwin's bottom line). In other words, we believe that both kinds of processes, effective courtship display mechanisms and cognitive mating mechanisms (that are directly related to mating issues), can independently lead to markers of mating success. An implication of this framework is the idea that there are multiple routes or strategies to Darwinian success, a point that matches a major theme of this book—that an evolutionary perspective emphasizes extraordinary flexibility in the strategies and qualities that lead to survival and reproduction. The idea of mating intelligence, which is a core aspect of psychology related to pair-bonding and other aspects of mating, helps us understand how this is possible.

SUMMARY: LONG-TERM HUMAN MATING

Monogamy has an important history in our species and long-term mating tactics are crucial in helping people achieve long-term reproductive success, largely given how altricial our young are. Choosing a long-term partner is a basic element of life from an evolutionary perspective, and our mate-choice psychology along with the psychology of relationships speak to the role of pair-bonding in the deep past of our species. Mating intelligence, which speaks to the entire set of cognitive processes that underlie human mating, is clearly shaped to help facilitate success in both short- and long-term mating contexts.

DISCUSSION/ESSAY EXERCISES

- Briefly describe how evolutionary psychologists explain the experience of love. Be sure to set your answer in the context of monogamy and pair-bonding. Also, relate your answer to issues of parental investment.
- Describe how infidelity is thought to be an *adaptive hurdle* in the mating domain. Also address how research has shown that men and women seem to experience different adaptive hurdles in regard to infidelity, and how men and women seem to respond differently to infidelity as a result.

- Describe the notion of cuckoldry and how this relates to paternal-assurance tactics. In your answer, describe at least three different paternal-assurance tactics that seem to have evolved to address the issue of cuckoldry.
- Briefly describe the concept of *mating intelligence*. In your answer, be sure to describe the concepts of *courtship display mechanisms* along with *mating mechanisms*. Finally, describe the idea of mating success and how mating intelligence is thought to relate to this important variable.

The Oftentimes-Helpful, Churchgoing Ape

KEY TERMS

- The altruism problem
- Inclusive fitness
- Direct versus indirect fitness
- Relatedness
- Reciprocal altruism
- Moral emotions
- Cheater detection
- Competitive altruism
- Sexually selected altruism
- Multilevel selection and altruism

CHAPTER 6

- Evolutionary accounts of religion
- Wilson's idea of the "horizontal" and "vertical" dimensions of religion

n the field of evolution, there are many paradoxes—things about the nature of life that seem to fly in the face of evolutionary principles, or things about life that simply make little sense from an evolutionary perspective. Perhaps the best-known example of such a phenomenon is *altruism*, generally defined as the helping of another organism at a cost to oneself. Think about it. If "evolution is right," and organisms that evolved and typify life on this planet are full of adaptations that facilitate their own reproductive success—why and how could altruism evolve?

This issue has become known as *the altruism problem* and, fortunately, as you'll see, examining this problem actually led to extraordinary advances—not only in our understanding of evolutionary processes, but in our understanding of altruism as well. In other words, the altruism problem didn't take down evolutionary theory. Rather, it bolstered evolutionary theory.

KIN-SELECTED ALTRUISM

William Hamilton, a renowned zoologist whose work in the 1960s revolutionized our understanding of evolution, was the first to make substantial headway in solving the altruism problem. At the time, Hamilton (1964) was studying several species described as the *social insects*. Social insects include many species of bees, wasps, ants, and other kinds of insects. The defining feature of a social insect species is the fact that individuals work together and function as something of a group organism—such as honeybees, with a hive including a queen and thousands of worker bees and drones that work in a coordinated fashion to obtain food, help build the nest, and so on.

In short, the social insects seem to show extraordinary levels of altruism, including behavior that is clearly for the benefit of the hive and/or the queen—often at a cost to the individual (with many species of social insects displaying kamikaze behaviors!).

So if you're an evolutionist and you study the social insects, you've got to wonder: How could these complicated and seemingly altruistic behaviors have evolved? Due to our understanding of genetics, there's an answer—and Hamilton was the first to document this connection between genetic constellations of particular species and patterns of altruistic behaviors. Hamilton's big insight is essentially this: The social insects have a different pattern of genetic relatedness to one another compared with other sexually reproducing species such as humans. Drones receive 100% of their genes from the queen—and workers will share 75% of their genes with one another (as opposed to the 50% of shared genes that humans share with full siblings).

So here's the connection that inspired Hamilton's big insight—perhaps relatively high levels of genetic interrelatedness among individuals within a species relates in an important way to the amount of altruism we expect to see within that species. And this idea relates importantly to Hamilton's theory of *inclusive fitness*. Inclusive fitness, described in the first chapter, suggests that there are two distinct methods by which an organism can increase its fitness or levels of reproductive success. One mechanism is *direct fitness*, by which an organism facilitates its own survival and/or reproduction. Separately, we can think of *indirect fitness*, which includes processes by which an organism facilitates the survival and/or reproductive ability of its *kin* (i.e., genetically related individuals).

Think about it. If the "goal" of a gene is to replicate itself, it can do so by facilitating its reproduction in the body in which it finds itself *or* it can facilitate its replication ability by somehow helping other organisms that share replicas of that particular gene. And which organisms are likely to share replicas of a particular gene? Kin. Helping with the reproductive success of kin is, essentially and importantly, helping with the reproductive success of one's own genes.

While we share genes with all organisms, kin are individuals with whom we share a disproportionately high amount of genes. This is why idiosyncratic things tend to run in families. My older brother is nearly 6 feet tall, and he's considered a giant in our family. My wife and her sister both have a small gap between their two front teeth—so does my mother-in-law, and my two kids, and their cousins on my wife's side.

Evolution is a large-scale optimization process. Genes that have been selected over thousands of generations are genes that essentially are good at creating phenotypes that in turn are somehow good at getting replicas of those genes into the future. Genes that code for behavioral patterns that lead to favored helping—biasing individuals toward helping genetically related kin—would be genes that would outcompete other genes because, indirectly but importantly, they are good at getting replicas of themselves into the future.

Belding's ground squirrels that live in the woods of the Pacific Northwest are amazing. Sherman (1985) has studied their social behavior in detail and has documented very clear evidence for the existence of kin-selected altruism in studying these animals. Ground squirrels are like arboreal squirrels that you might be more familiar with but they don't go up trees. They find shelter in piles of wood and rocks on the forest floor.

As is often the case, there are predators! Predators of ground squirrels include wild cats, hawks, coyotes, and more. So they often have reason to scramble under the rocks. Under some conditions, a ground squirrel will let out a loud screech just before dashing to safety in the presence of a predator. On the surface, this seems like a bad idea! Not only does this *distress call* take time and energy, but it also is conspicuous, drawing attention to the animal making the call. Why would a squirrel do this? It doesn't seem to make much sense from an evolutionary perspective.

And, as you may have guessed, this is where Hamilton's ideas of inclusive fitness and kin-selected altruism save the day!

In his work on these animals, Sherman explored the possible role of kin selection by examining (a) which other squirrels are present when a distress call is made and (b) how related these squirrels are to the animal that makes the distress call. The answer ends up being very straightforward—if a high proportion of genetic kin is in the area, the probability of a distress call is high. If the proportion of genetic kin in the area is low, the probability of a distress call is low. And as more highly related kin are close (e.g., sons, daughters, and siblings, who are ".5" relatives [sharing 50% of genetic combinations with an individual]) compared with less-related kin (such as nieces and nephews (.25 r [or *relatedness*]), the likelihood of emitting this kind of call goes down. The story is very clear. This kind of self-sacrificial, apparently altruistic act emerges as a mechanism to help foster the survival and reproduction of kin—who, by definition, share genes with oneself.

In a similar line of research, Wolfenden and Fitzpatrick (1984) found evidence for kin-selected altruism in the Florida scrub jay (which appears as very similar to their relatives, the blue jay). Scrub jays mate in densely populated marshy areas and there tend to not be enough resources for all adults in a population to successfully mate and produce offspring directly. But as is the case with many bird species, the young of the scrub jay are altricial—needing a lot of adult support to be able to acquire enough food to survive. Two parents are often not enough to feed a full nest of hatchlings successfully given the intensive metabolism of the developing young. So this species has evolved a form of extra-parental help in rearing young. And the question here is, essentially, who helps? From a strict selfish gene perspective, helping the young of others is time not spent helping the young of yourself and it doesn't make clear sense how this could be naturally selected—not on the surface, in any case.

Kin-selected altruism, again, explains this phenomenon. Helpers at the nest are not random adults in the population; they tend to be kin or genetic relatives of the young. Further, the closer the kin relationship, for example, being an uncle (with r of .25), compared with an adult cousin (with r of .125), corresponds to a higher amount of helping. Helping others is often kin-selected altruism—and this is, ultimately, helping one's own genes as they exist in the bodies of others.

And kin-selected altruism exists in humans, too! First off, think about the role of mothers in our species. As we've discussed in several chapters, mothers inherently pay high costs in reproducing. Pregnancy, childbirth, nursing—these all take an extraordinary amount of time and energy—let alone the work that goes into being a mother across a child's full development. The most prevalent kind of altruism—or helping behavior—in our species is mothering, by far and away. And kin selection can help us understand why this is so. Helping one's offspring is perhaps the most direct form of helping one's genes as they exist in the body of another.

In studies of kin-selected altruism in humans, Bernstein (2005) and Garvey, Brosseau, and Jennings (2012) have documented that our decision-making processes seem strongly related to issues of kinship. In a social psychological study of targets of altruistic acts, Bernstein et al. created situations where help would be needed—such as helping someone with groceries or helping someone get out of a burning building. And the targets of the altruistic acts were manipulated in terms of kinship (the person to be helped was either a stranger or a family member with varying degrees of kin relatedness). The short version of the findings is as follows: People reported being more willing to help genetic relatives compared with others. In humans, kinship is a strong predictor of helping behavior.

In a set of "trolley car" studies, Garvey and his colleagues (2012) examined kin-selected altruism from a different angle. In "trolley car" research, a participant is presented with a specific kind of social/moral judgment. The idea is that you imagine you have control over the changing of the tracks of a trolley car. And a certain number of people are stuck on one track and a certain number of folks are stuck on the other track. And it's up to you to pull the switch to determine which track the trolley takes and who "gets it." Using this methodology, Garvey and his colleagues added a twist to this research by not only manipulating the number of individuals on each track but by also manipulating the relatedness of the individuals (e.g., track #1 could have three of your siblings while track #2 could have seven strangers). Consistent with past research on the role of kin selection in social behavior, the results were clear—people are more likely to save kin, particularly if the kin relations are close. In fact, people are likely to help kin at a cost to nonkin, being willing to let several strangers die to save a few kin. This research speaks to our environment of evolutionary adaptedness and the fact that helping kin was an important aspect of social behavior of our ancestors—and this kind of helping was naturally selected. Further, and more simply, this research speaks to the evolutionary psychology of nepotism. It helps us understand the "problem of nepotism" from an evolutionary perspective.

RECIPROCAL ALTRUISM

While kin selection explains a huge proportion of helping behavior that we see in the world, it hardly explains it all. We know from experience that people help nonkin all the time! Evolutionary psychologists have come up with many explanations of nonkin altruism. And it turns out that evolutionary explanations can help us understand many forms of non–kin-selected altruism.

The most commonly studied form of nonkin altruism has been *reciprocal altruism*. Rooted in another seminal theory by Robert Trivers (1971), reciprocal altruism is the idea that you help someone with an expectation of being helped in return. This expectation need not be conscious, and this form of mutually beneficial helping need not be constrained to humans. In chimpanzees, as in humans (see Nelson & Geher, 2006), individuals groom one another—often removing dangerous parasites. Importantly, in chimpanzees, parasite removal is based on reciprocity. Chimps base the decision of whether to groom another or not on whether that other has helped him or her in the past (de Waal, 1989).

In vampire bats, an interesting form of reciprocal altruism takes place. These animals go out to get the blood of mammals—and return to share this feast with others by regurgitating some of the blood for others to share (Wilkinson, 1984). I know—gross! In any case, they don't just share this blood with any old bat—they are selective, being more likely to provide this tasty treat for both (a) kin and (b) unrelated individuals who have helped them in the past. Cooperative alliances seem to be an important feature of the evolved social structure of vampire bats.

In true Trivers fashion, reciprocal altruism theory includes some basic axioms that make strong evolutionary sense and that seem to work amazingly well in typifying behavior across various species. For a species to be able to have reciprocal altruism evolve, that species must have the following three features (Trivers, 1985):

1. A relatively long life span.
2. The ability to identify conspecifics.
3. A tendency to live in relatively stable groups.

All these features essentially create a chance that altruistic acts can be paid back. Because only if this is the case can it evolve in a way that allows such acts to benefit an individual altruist. Think about it. If an animal doesn't have a long life span, then an altruistic act can't be paid back because by the time the potential reciprocal altruist is ready to pay back some help, the original animal is dead. Also, the ability to identify specific conspecifics is important—if you receive help from someone and you'd love to help that individual back but are not able to tell who is who (as is the case in some species), then you just can't pay back that favor! Also, if you owe someone a favor but you don't live in stable groups, you may never see that individual again—whoops! Meant to pay back, but it just wasn't feasible!

And, in fact, as has often been the case historically, Trivers is right. Reciprocal altruism has only evolved in species that fit the above criteria.

And, of course, humans fit these criteria very well—we live long lives, we can easily identify individuals (in fact, human face recognition abilities seem exceptional, which may result from our deep history of reciprocal altruism [see Fiske & Taylor, 1990]), and we live in relatively stable groups. And reciprocal altruism is rampant in our species.

In fact, Trivers points out that many of the human emotions seem integrally tied to issues of reciprocal altruism. We feel proud when we help another. We feel ashamed when we fail to reciprocate altruism. We express being apologetic to others if we mean to help them out but don't do so. We feel outraged when we find out that someone who has received a great deal of help from others fails to help others back. In his analysis of human emotions from an evolutionary perspective, Trivers (1985) makes a strong case that issues of reciprocal altruism may play a major role in helping us understand the nature of human emotions.

In a tantalizing follow-up idea regarding the importance of reciprocal altruism in our broader human psychology, Trivers suggests that basic human mathematical abilities may be rooted in reciprocal altruism, with the idea that the most basic human math may be counting acts of helping: Who have I helped? Who "owes me?" Who has helped me? How much? Who do I owe? I shared food with her three times and she hasn't shared with me at all. And so forth.

In a social world in which reciprocal altruism is prevalent, we benefit from psychologies that help us monitor the behaviors of others to see who is a *helper* and who is a *cheater* or *social loafer*. We also benefit from psychologies that allow us to monitor ourselves, to make sure that we're contributing appropriately and to help make sure that our own reputation as a reciprocal altruist within the group is positive.

As you can see, Trivers' theory of reciprocal altruism has enormous potential to help us understand why people help nonkin as well as why the human emotional and cognitive systems are shaped as they are. Why are people the way they are? Partly because reciprocal altruism is a major feature of human social systems—and it has been for eons.

CHEATER DETECTION

Trivers' ideas on reciprocal altruism largely focus on people who *cheat*, those who take benefits from others without reciprocating. Such individuals inflict costs to one's broader social community as well as to oneself. As such, the ability to detect cheaters should be an important element of human psychology to the extent that reciprocal altruism is a major part of who we are.

With this evolutionarily informed reasoning in hand, Cosmides and Tooby (1992) focus on the psychology of detecting individuals who cheat on social contracts—that is, agreements between people that are made in some explicit manner. If someone cheats on a social contract, that behavior signals that this person may not reciprocate altruism—and this would be important information in social life.

Their specific hypothesis essentially is that we have specialized cognitive abilities tied to detecting cheaters in the context of social contracts. All things equal, we should be better at using logic to detect people who cheat on social contracts than in other kinds of situations.

To test this hypothesis, these researchers used a standard logic task employed by cognitive psychologists—the Wason Selection Task (1966). In this task, people are presented with an if/then kind of situation and are asked to make logical judgments accordingly. Importantly, the logic involved in the task doesn't change even if the content of the question changes.

In a standard version of this task, participants are provided with a scenario about a clerical-filing task. They are told something such as if a file has a 7 on the label, they need to file it under F. They are then presented with four cards—each with a number on one side and a letter on the other. They are asked which cards they need to turn over to see if the rule has been violated. An example of what the cards in this scenario look like is found in Table 6.1.

So here, students have to figure out which cards might provide information to see if the rule has been violated. In Cosmides and Tooby's (1992) research using this example, about a third of a large sample of undergraduate (Stanford Univeristy) students got the correct answer—most didn't.

Which cards did you pick? If you chose 7 and *D*, you're right! If you chose something else, don't feel bad—you're in good company with the students at Stanford who failed this one!

If you're like most students I know, you're frustrated now— and you're thinking "No way—that's not the right answer . . . this wasn't worded correctly . . ." or something like that. Honestly, this is almost like a good party trick—works almost every time. Here's the deal. In the task you're given, you're only asked specifically to make sure that something labeled 7 is filed under F. Well the card with the 7 on it is relevant, because if it has something other than an F on the other side, that's a violation. The next one, with D on it, needs to be considered, because if that has a 7 on other side, it was misfiled. The F doesn't matter—because whatever number is on the other side is fine; 7 *has* to go in F, but based on the information you're given, labels with other numbers can certainly be filed as F as well. And if there's a 3, then who cares! Whatever is on the other side will not bear on the issue of the rule you're being asked to examine.

But that problem doesn't have much to do with a social contract, now does it? Consider this scenario, which might be more meaningful to you and which relates to a social contract

TABLE 6.1 **CARDS USED IN A STANDARD WASON SELECTION TASK**

Instructions: Each card has a letter on one side and a number on the other. Please indicate which of the following cards need to be turned over to see if the rule described in the clerical-filing task scenario has been violated.

7	D	F	3

that millions of college students are aware of. Scenario: You're a bouncer at the cool bar in town. Your boss gives you a simple rule—to make sure that if someone's drinking beer, that person's ID indicates that he or she is 21 or older. Refer to Table 6.2 for the cards related to this task. As in the prior example, your task is to determine which cards need to be turned over to see if the rule has been violated.

Importantly, the underlying logic in this example is identical to the logic in the other (standard) example. However, if you're like most people, you find this one easier. What did you choose? If you chose *Beer* and *16*, you're right! A majority of students in Cosmides and Tooby's (1992) research get this one right. If the person's 21, you don't need to check what the person is drinking. If the person's drinking soda, it doesn't matter how old the person is. But if the person's drinking beer, you need to know how old that person is—and if the person's 16, you better know what that person is drinking.

Most people find this second example much easier than the first example, in spite of the fact that the underlying logic is identical. In a series of detailed studies on this topic, Cosmides and Tooby (1992) systematically documented the importance of social-contract relevance on these kinds of judgments. The second example relates to an important social contract—or rule between people in our society—that you need to be 21 or older to drink alcohol. The first example, about a mundane clerical task, does not relate to a social contract. In Cosmides and Tooby's (1992) research, many examples of social-contract–relevant scenarios are provided—and people consistently do better on these than on identical logic tasks that are not relevant to social contracts.

TABLE 6.2 **CARDS USED IN A SOCIAL-CONTRACT-RELEVANT WASON SELECTION TASK**

Instructions: Each card has a kind of drink on one side and the age of the person on the other side. Please indicate which of the following cards need to be turned over to see if the rule described in the social-contract scenario has been violated.

21	Beer	16	Soda

Cosmides and Tooby's (1992) research on social contracts is important, because it shows how the ideas extrapolated from Trivers' (1971) reciprocal altruism theory can be operationalized and studied in a way that sheds light on basic psychological processes such as foundational logic abilities.

COMPETITIVE ALTRUISM, SEXY ALTRUISM, AND THE POSSIBILITY OF GENUINE ALTRUISM

To this point, our evolutionarily informed dissection of altruism has been pretty powerful. We've examined the role of kinship and the role of reciprocal altruism in helping us understand the *altruism problem*. But you know, in reality, we haven't addressed altruism at all via this analysis! That is, both the ideas of kin-selected altruism and reciprocal altruism ultimately talk about benefits to the individual that flow from *apparently altruistic* acts. That is, these theories really paint a portrait of helpful acts in our species as being ultimately selfish and not altruistic at all when it comes down to it!

For this reason, evolutionary psychology is sometimes portrayed as presenting a sort of nasty take on humanity—seeing people as ultimately, importantly, and always selfish. Yes, I guess I can see why people might not like that so much.

Until very recently—perhaps up until about 2000, the basic answer to the altruism problem presented by evolutionary psychologists really did revolve around kin-related altruism and reciprocal altruism. To be fair, the delineation of these classes of altruism—and their connections with an evolutionary understanding of behavior—have led to huge advancements in the understanding of psychology across species. And in combination, it's fair to say that kin-selected altruism and reciprocal altruism comprise an enormous amount of the prosocial behaviors that exist in humans and other species.

In recent years, however, some great evolutionarily inspired research has led to advancements in our understanding of altruism beyond the bounds of kin selection and reciprocal altruism. Two such advances, included in this section, are the phenomena of *competitive altruism* (Barclay, 2011) and altruism as a courtship device (Miller, 2007). While these classes of altruism don't necessarily paint a full picture of the existence of genuine altruism, you'll see that they help move the discussion in that direction.

How much we help others partly depends on how much others help. If you've ever been to a fundraiser, you've seen this in action. For a good cause, such as supporting the local library or a foundation dedicated to fighting cancer, people will outbid one another in buying raffle tickets or bidding on items in an auction—all to benefit a worthy and altruistic cause. In a series of systematic studies on this topic, Barclay demonstrated strong evidence that, when framed appropriately, a competitive context can really facilitate prosocial acts. Winning competitions leads to status elevation, and to resultant fitness benefits. Competitive altruism is another form of altruism that can be explained by an evolutionary perspective.

Miller's (2007) theory of altruism as sexually selected is similar. In a major rethinking of evolutionary psychology, recall that Miller developed his theory of mental fitness indicators, suggesting that creative psychological processes such as musical abilities, intelligence, and humor, evolved and have become species typical because they serve an important function in attracting mates. In several thought-provoking chapters and articles, Miller has made a strong case for the idea that altruism in humans may also have evolved for the purposes of attracting mates. Sure, this sounds kind of cold—and perhaps a bit weird—at first, but in a major synthesis of research on this topic, Miller (2007) makes a strong case.

For one, markers of altruism are consistently rated as important features in potential mates. Kindness, helpfulness, other-orientedness—these are all things we want in mates and these desires are universal (Buss et al., 1989). From a straightforward sexual selection perspective, if a feature is desired by members of the opposite sex, this feature will be selected. Further, the basic personality traits that underlie things such as kindness—including agreeableness—seem to have at least some heritable component. So when people select mates for kindness and agreeableness, they are indirectly selecting genes that code for these features in future generations of people.

Altruism is attractive in mates for several basic reasons. Someone who displays altruism is likely going to be nice to you as a partner and is likely to be kind and giving to any shared offspring that you may have. Further, Miller argues that conspicuous acts of altruism are often done for social display purposes. Anonymous donations exist, but they are not as common as donations with names attached to them. And as Miller insightfully points out, an individual who gives a major anonymous gift for an altruistic cause probably informs his or her romantic partner of the situation.

Now we get to the issue of genuine altruism. To the extent that markers of altruism, such as kindness, are displayed in mating contexts, people should be wary of dishonest or disingenuine displays of kindness. We discriminate between what we consider *genuine* kindness versus someone who's *just saying that* or is *just acting that way*. In fact, much research on the nature of social deception has shown that deception in the mating domain is very prevalent, and that much of our mating intelligence is focused on efforts to discern honest from dishonest mating signals (O'Sullivan, 2008).

So we're motivated not only to display kindness, but to display genuine kindness. And what's the best way to display genuine kindness and tendencies toward altruism? If you're genuinely kind and altruistic, you don't need to exert time and effort into faking it! Through this route, the sexual-selection take on altruism may actually hold a key to the evolutionary roots of genuine altruism.

MULTILEVEL SELECTION, RELIGION, AND GOD

In another major initiative to help shed light on the evolution of altruism, David Sloan Wilson (2007) has used his theory of multilevel selection to help us understand the nature of altruism and the role of religion in what it means to be human. Recall that multilevel selection focuses on how selection can act at multiple levels—at the level of a gene, a cell, a part of an organism, an organism, a group of kin, or a group of nonrelated individuals who form a social unit with benefits to the individual members.

In terms of altruism, Wilson's ideas are very useful in thinking about the importance of non–kin-based social groups that function like an organism. In fact, such groups are very basic to human social functioning, and it seems that our tendency to form groups beyond kin lines is one of the basic aspects of human social psychology. Some theories have suggested that the main difference between humans and Neanderthals pertains to our ability to form cooperative alliances with nonkin—something that the Neanderthals seemed to have never done (which may account for why their brains were larger than ours, but they went extinct about 40,000 years ago; Hodgson, Bergey, & Disotell, 2010).

Humans form groups that extend beyond kin lines—and think about what this allows us to do! We can form communities, cities, civilizations, and more. We can build bridges, create universities, and put a man on the moon. None of these extraordinary outcomes would be possible without large-scale cooperation that cuts beyond kin lines. Such cooperation surely speaks to altruism among individuals who are unrelated. And it makes sense from a selection perspective. If I'm part of a group that is highly successful, I can help the group with its success, and success will flow down my way as well.

In some classic research in social psychology, Tajfel (1981) found something amazing. People automatically and easily form *ingroups* and *outgroups*—defined as people that are "in my group" or not. Why is this amazing? Because it's so remarkably basic to our psychology. People define others as ingroup or outgroup members, literally, at the flip of a coin. If you and I both flip heads, and someone else flips tails, research shows that we may actually treat one another positively and that we may be not-so-nice to that dude who flipped tails. People form ingroups based on all kinds of criteria—ethnic group, regional affiliation, college affiliation, area of academic major, and more. And, importantly, people form ingroups and outgroups based on religion.

In his treatise on religion from an evolutionary perspective titled *Darwin's Cathedral*, David Sloan Wilson (2002) focuses on religions as large-scale ingroups that evolved to promote altruism within groups. Being part of a successful religion benefits an individual as it helps that individual gain the benefits of the group. Further, among competing religious groups, some groups outlast others. These groups that are selected at this level bring individuals along for the ride—and this is the core of multilevel selection.

In Wilson's analysis of many religious groups across the world, several common themes emerged regarding what religions are all about. So while religions seem to differ dramatically from one another in the details (dress this way, eat this but not that, pray at this time of day, worship this god, etc.), they actually share many common structural elements. Successful religious groups are filled with rules that get people to inhibit selfish needs and contribute to the needs of the greater good. And think about these rules. Don't kill. Honor your parents. Don't steal. These are all things that have to do with facilitating positive behaviors within the group. To some extent, these kinds of rules are about social control—keeping people in line—and getting people to put the broader group interests ahead of selfish interests. While these kinds of rules may not help an individual in the immediate term, they help the group—and the individual—in the long-term, because they ensure that others in the group are less likely to inflict costs on that individual. If I know that you're part of my same religious group and I know that you follow the same rules that we all follow, then I can count on you not killing me, not stealing from me, not sleeping with my wife, and so forth. This is a pretty good deal! So the individual ultimately and importantly benefits from being part of this group.

When it comes to religion and evolution, the famous discussions that have taken place have focused on these institutions' conflicts with one another. Richard Dawkins (2006), author of *The God Delusion*, is famous for arguing that religion is simply inaccurate in its depiction of reality and that it is up to modern, enlightened individuals to spread a secular and humane message to members of cultures across the globe. And this is typical of what evolutionists have to say on the topic of religion.

A separate, and perhaps more productive, angle on the interface of evolution and religion is found in work on the evolutionary origins and functions of religion. As Wilson puts it, any religion can be divided into two basic elements or dimensions. Wilson talks about the vertical dimension as related to people's connection with the supernatural, and the horizontal dimension as related to people's connections with one another. The vertical dimension is conceptualized as a proximate element of religion—the specific, immediate way that religious groups exert an influence over individuals. Recall that proximate causes of behaviors are those immediate and specific causes. For instance, a religious Christian may decide to not steal a piece of food, even though he's hungry, because he's thinking that God would find out and he'd really rather not go to Hell when he dies. So these supernatural features of religion can be conceptualized as the proximate ways that a religion exerts influence over an individual.

For Wilson (2007), the ultimate cause of religion pertains to social control—inhibiting selfish behaviors and promoting behaviors that are good for the group. This *horizontal dimension* is, for Wilson, the reason that religion came to characterize humans and is the reason that religion is an important part of our evolutionary heritage. From this perspective, religion evolved because it helped our ancestors form cooperative groups that cut beyond kin lines and provided important long-term benefits to individual members.

Religious behavior, then, is, in an important sense, a dominant form of altruistic behavior that expands across human cultures. Certainly altruism and moral behavior can exist separate from specific religions in modern contexts. But given the deep roots that religion has in the evolutionary history of our species, it's clear that understanding the ultimate causes of religion helps us to understand the ultimate causes of altruism.

As is the case with sexually selected forms of altruism (per Miller's [2007] theory), Wilson's multilevel selection take on altruism also opens the door for a discussion of the existence of genuine altruism. If people evolved to be part of non–kin-based cooperative groups, then individuals within such groups who were genuine in having the interests of the group in mind would have the capacity to benefit the group—with the interests of themselves and their kin being supported along the way.

SUMMARY: THE DIFFERENT PIECES OF HUMAN ALTRUISM

The altruism problem, which initially emerged as a major intellectual obstacle for evolutionists, has led to extraordinary advances in our understanding of social behavior across species. From Hamilton's theories on kin-selected altruism, Trivers' theory of reciprocal altruism, Barclay's work on competitive altruism, Miller's work on sexually selected altruism, and Wilson's work on altruism as rooted in multilevel selection processes, modern evolutionary psychology has many tools that allow for an explanation of the existence of prosocial, other-oriented behavior. And in combination, these theories open the door to discussions of the existence of genuine altruism.

DISCUSSION/ESSAY EXERCISES

● Briefly describe "the altruism problem" as it relates to evolution. Next, describe kin-selection theory and how this theory and its correlate "inclusive fitness" address how evolution can account for altruism.

● Describe Trivers' (1971) theory of reciprocal altruism. In your answer, describe the three basic characteristics of a species that must exist for reciprocal altruism to characterize that species. Finally, describe Trivers' speculative idea that mathematical reasoning has its roots in issues surrounding reciprocal altruism.

● Describe Cosmides and Tooby's (1992) basic methodological paradigm regarding cheater detection. Explain how this research is rooted in Trivers' ideas of reciprocal altruism and Dunbar's ideas on our ancestors having small social groups. In your answer, describe basic findings from Cosmides and Tooby's work that support the idea of a "specialized cheater-detection module."

● Describe Miller's (2000) idea that altruism serves a courtship-related function. In your answer, describe what he has to say on the idea of altruism being sexy. Finally, describe one example he raises (conceptual or research-based) that speaks to this idea of altruism being an effective courtship display mechanism.

● Describe Wilson's (2007) summary of religion. In your explanation, describe what he means by the "horizontal" and "vertical" dimensions of religion. Further, explain how he describes each of these dimensions as serving as a basis for a "successful" religion. Finally, describe what Wilson means by a "successful" religion, particularly in terms of his idea of multilevel selection.

Aggression, Warfare, and Human Nastiness

KEY TERMS

- Evolutionarily based equilibria
- Gloved-fisted view of aggression
- "Hawks and doves"
- Game theory
- Sexual selection and aggression
- Sexual dimorphism
- Adaptive theories of homicide and murder
- Naturalistic fallacy
- "Spoils of war"
- Dehumanization of the enemy
- Remote killing capacities
- Projectile weapons
- The relationship between remote killing and the rise of egalitarianism

From an evolutionary perspective, aggression is less mysterious on the surface when compared with altruism. If organisms are shaped by evolutionary forces to facilitate their own reproductive success, helping conspecifics makes little apparent sense, while hurting conspecifics to benefit oneself makes more apparent sense. Therefore, from an evolutionary perspective, aggressive tendencies make sense. That being said, unfettered and random aggression, as we'll see, makes little evolutionary sense and, as a result, is not an accurate characterization of human social behavior.

As is true across many species, aggression exists in humans, but the nature of aggression and its details tell a story of human aggression as existing in highly specified ways and contexts— contexts that make sense from an evolutionary perspective.

CONCEPTUAL PERSPECTIVES ON AGGRESSION: HAWKS AND DOVES

If human behavior were completely about benefiting oneself at a cost to conspecifics, then we would likely expect people to always be highly aggressive to all other humans—except, perhaps, to potential and actual mates and offspring and other kin members. While human social behavior is not always beautiful, this rampant-aggresion portrait hardly characterizes what we see in human social worlds. Instead, we actually see very few acts of physical aggression between individuals on a day-to-day basis.

Sometimes, we see posturing or play-fighting, such as kids wrestling around when playing. In fact, this kind of play-fighting is very common in the development of the young of many species

(Lorenz, 1963) and has led to the idea that aggressive tendencies in animals really doesn't serve the function of inflicting harm on conspecifics.

In a detailed treatise on the nature of aggression, Dawkins (1976, connecting with the work of Axelrod, 1984) talks about aggression in terms of *game theory*. Game theory is essentially the idea of trade-offs that we discussed in the first chapter. All acts that come with evolutionary benefits may come with evolutionary costs as well. For instance, time spent courting an attractive mate may lead to evolutionary benefits of successful reproduction, but these same acts may lead to time spent courting that could be spend on other important life domains—and it may not end up being successful (sometimes, suitors are rejected). So, as discussed many times in this book, there are always trade-offs.

In analyzing aggressive behaviors, the idea of trade-offs comes strongly into play. And this can be translated into game theory. Game theory essentially sees individuals as players in a game—with the goal of trying to optimize their own particular lot (such as, in evolutionary terms, trying to optimize one's own genetic fitness). In any game, optimizing your own lot—or "trying to win"—requires strategy and needs to take many factors into account. In the game Monopoly, for instance, if you try to optimize your situation by buying any and all property no matter what, you will lose money and you may end up losing the game because you optimized along one dimension (properties) but not along other relevant dimensions (money). From an evolutionary perspective, all aspects of life—of all organisms—have this same game-like quality.

When it comes to aggression, there are costs and benefits—trade-offs—regarding aggressive behaviors. Acting aggressively toward a conspecific may lead you to take that individual out of the running and lead you to get whatever resources are available, but there is always the chance of you losing a physical altercation and of running into other adverse consequences.

For instance, consider two young males who belong to different tribes. They both find a game animal and they each want to bring it back to their tribe for dinner. Well, they may fight one another for access to it. If they're about evenly matched in terms of size, this is a scary proposition. In fact, it's a scary proposition in any case. Suppose one grabs the food and a fight breaks out. Punches, kicks, sticks, and stones all come into the picture. Easily, one of these individuals could die. Now that's a major evolutionary cost! And severe injury is a possibility for each of them. So the benefits of winning the resource need to be balanced in light of the potential costs.

The concept of *hawks* and *doves* has been used to explicate this idea (Axelrod, 1984). This idea speaks not to different species, but rather, it speaks metaphorically to different behavioral strategies regarding issues of aggression. In this framework, a *hawk* is an individual who always behaves aggressively while a *dove* is an individual who never behaves aggressively. These extreme behavioral strategies each have general costs and benefits associated with them. A hawk will always do well against a dove—winning whatever resource is at stake. But a hawk will often do poorly against another hawk with the risk of death or physical injury as possible outcomes.

Meanwhile, while a dove does poorly against a hawk, it never does *too poorly* because it doesn't get hurt as it never fights (it retreats). A dove can do fine against another dove (perhaps one retreats over time—perhaps they split the resource). So out-and-out, unconditional aggression in the form of an extreme hawk-like strategy is, in fact, not the evolutionarily optimal strategy in terms of acquiring needed resources.

Mathematical models have been applied to help us understand such game-like scenarios and such models end up with solutions that speak to *evolutionarily based equilibria*; that is, ratios of each kind of strategy that are optimized to the point such that the expected average evolutionary payout for one strategy is equal to the expected average payout for the alternative strategy. So depending on the costs and benefits of relevant variables (such as the cost of physical injury, the benefit of acquiring the resource, etc.), the ratio of hawks to doves in a population will be determined—and will, across multiple generations, arrive at a stable equilibrium point such that it will pay, on average, just as much to be a hawk as it does to be a dove.

While the hawk and dove metaphor here seems to speak to unconditional and discrete phenotypes, as Dawkins (1976) points out, this metaphor works just as well to conceptualize ratios of hawk- and dove-like behaviors within an individual's own strategic repertoire. If an optimal ratio, for instance, based on the mathematical details, is 50% hawks and 50% doves, then this model can either predict that half the individuals in a population will display hawk-like behavior while the other half will display dove-like behavior. Or this model could predict that all members of the population utilize a hawk-like strategy 50% of the time (on average) and that all members of the population use a dove-like strategy 50% of the time (on average).

The parameters demarcated in this example are abstract, but they help make a point. In such a population with these mathematical parameters (which are clearly somewhat arbitrary and designed to make a point), we can see how unconstrained aggression would actually be selected against (as would unconstrained pacifism). A mixed strategy is, in this case, optimal. And when it comes to evolutionarily shaped behavioral strategies, this is often the case.

This example of hawks and doves helps us understand some basic issues regarding the evolution of aggression. A simple "aggression is always selected" algorithm is simply misinformed and doesn't match the ecological complexity of the real worlds that animals find themselves residing in.

In short, this all suggests that aggression has been selected—but within real and important parameters. Too much aggression can be just as evolutionarily detrimental as too little. And game theory, a core aspect of the theoretical component of evolutionary psychology, helps us understand the complexities regarding this important aspect of social behavior.

GLOVED-FISTED AGGRESSION

In his renowned treatise on aggression (literally titled *On Aggression*), Konrad Lorenz (1963) analyzed aggression in many species of animals—from giraffes to snakes to elk—and came to a conclusion that points to a *gloved-fisted* view of aggression across animal species. His main conclusion, consistent with the game-theory analysis already discussed, is that most aggression between conspecifics is actually not designed to hurt or to kill. Most aggression ends up being posturing—tests of strengths in competitions that rarely lead to serious injury or death. Bull elk clash horns for a bit—but at the end of the day, they usually stop fighting and everyone walks away unharmed.

This is called a "gloved-fisted" approach as gloves help dampen the adverse effects of the punch of a fist (as in boxing). Why would such gloved-fisted aggression typify aggressive behavioral patterns across animal species? Game theory helps tell us why—all-out aggression designed to kill at all costs ends up being a strategy that rarely wins out in the end. Thank goodness!

AGGRESSION AND SEXUAL SELECTION

This having been said, we still have questions when we think about bull elk clashing horns. Can't they find something better to do with their time? Sexual dimorphism, or size and morphological differences (such as the presence of large antlers), exist in many species and this fact tells a story of intrasexual competition. In a species where one sex is much larger than the other, this is often a clue about the evolutionary history of that species. Typically, when we see such sexual dimorphism, we can guess that the larger sex includes a behavioral repertoire of physical fighting for access to members of the other sex. Why do bull elk fight with one another at all? Because the victors obtain access to females. Why would a male lion possibly pick a fight with a dominant, harem-holding other male (I sure wouldn't!)? Again, access to females.

Think about humans. Males are larger than females by about 15% (see Gallup & Frederick, 2010). Males are more muscular than females and are more designed for physical feats of strength (Bingham & Souza, 2009). From an evolutionary perspective, we can surmise on this information alone, then, that in our ancestral past, males have engaged in male/male competition for access to females. In such a scenario, there would be selection for size and muscularity in males, as males who won these altercations would have been more likely to have become our ancestors, and being larger and more muscular, would be predictive of winning such physical altercations. Across generations, such a selective process would lead to males being larger and more muscular than females. Simple selection—a basic evolutionary process.

In fact, male morphology (see Gallup & Frederick, 2010) and hormonal physiology, including increased testosterone levels relative to female levels, are fully consistent with the fact that males are relatively physically aggressive compared with females (see Buss, 2003). Consistent with our hawks and doves analysis, males rarely kill each other over access to females, but sometimes they actually do (Buss, 2005). In humans, aggression is not a small detail and aggression is largely a male thing. And a deep understanding of how sexual selection works helps us understand why.

THE MURDERER NEXT DOOR

In a shocking expose on the nature of human aggression, Buss (2005) tells a chilling account of research that speaks to murder and homicide as possible adaptations in our species. Murder and homicide within a species are rare—but in humans, these things are found across cultures around the globe. And homicide is a major cause of death in cities around the world (Daly & Wilson, 1988), again, speaking to the fact that aggression leading to mortality is a significant feature of humanity.

As Buss (2005) points out, successful murder comes with clear adaptive benefits. First, murder often takes out an intrasexual competitor. Reducing the competition, at least on a surface level, can have clear adaptive benefits for oneself. Further, in addition to eliminating one's competition, killing a competitor removes the possibility of that competitor's offspring competing with one's own offspring—so the future competition for one's own lineage actually benefits from the killing of an intrasexual competitor. Consistent with this conception of the evolutionary psychology of homicide and murder, it turns out that same-sex individuals who are similar in age to the murderer actually are often the targets of killing in humans—supporting the idea of murder and homicide as adaptations designed to take intrasexual competitors out of the pool of individuals competing for mates.

Consistent with this conception of homicide and murder, consider Daly, Wilson, and Weghorst's (1982) research, discussed previously, which shows that one of the most common contexts for homicide relates to sexual infidelity and men killing others whom they suspect of being with their partners sexually. Such a scenario clearly speaks to murder as having a function of taking out intrasexual competitors.

Importantly, at this point it's worth noting what we call the *naturalistic fallacy* (see Pinker, 2003), which exists when someone sees something framed by someone else as *natural* and then conflates this as the way things *should* be. We get into the naturalistic fallacy in more detail in the subsequent chapter that deals with controversies in evolutionary psychology. This said, it's worth raising this point here. Scholars like Buss and Daly and Wilson who study homicide from an evolutionary perspective are, importantly, not condoning homicide and murder. Rather, these scholars are using evolutionarily informed approaches to human behavior to help us better understand these important social issues. Understanding murder is much different from justifying murder. Using evolutionary psychology to help us understand murder as a natural phenomenon is a far cry from justifying this as an acceptable behavior—and to accuse evolutionists of justifying homicide and murder due to their conducting this research is, in effect, committing the naturalistic fallacy. Again, we'll get into this issue in more detail in the subsequent chapter dealing explicitly with controversies in the field.

THE EVOLUTIONARY PSYCHOLOGY OF WARFARE

Renowned primatologist Richard Wrangham (2010) found something amazing when he lived among the chimpanzees in Africa. Not only do our closest-living relatives commit murder by forming coalitions of males who will implement a sneak attack to find, kill, and eat a young chimp from a neighboring community, but Wrangham also documented all-male coalitions of chimpanzees planning full-scale, war-like battles, leading to multiple deaths and the acquisition of territory and resources on behalf of the aggressive troop. Yes, that happens. And I agree, it's not pretty.

Chimps aside, the only other species that has ever been documented to engage in coordinated killing with goals such as acquiring resources for one group by taking said resources from another group are critters like us. At any moment in time—since the dawn of human history—some war has been going on somewhere (Pinker, 2012). Warfare, like it or not, seems to be a core feature of human behavior.

War was common when the Bible was written and many passages in the Bible speak to the acquisition of resources from other groups as a result of victory in war. In the Bible, the "spoils of war" often are demarcated as livestock and virgin women (see Smith, 2007). This said, it's clear that war seems importantly related to themes found in evolutionary psychology. Obtaining livestock and virgin females clearly speaks to obtaining resources that bear on survival and reproduction. War seems to be an important part of our evolutionary heritage.

In a significant analysis of the evolutionary psychology of war, titled *The Most Dangerous Animal*, David Livingstone Smith (2007) examines features of warfare looking for human universals in this domain. Many common themes emerged from this analysis, including:

- The initiation and implementation of warfare is almost exclusively a male-oriented endeavor.
- Warfare almost always includes situations in which groups are fighting over limited evolutionarily relevant resources.
- Rape of women of the opposing side is a remarkably common outcome that corresponds to warfare.
- War nearly always includes the tendency for groups to psychologically dehumanize the opposition.

War is Hell—and evolutionary psychology can help us understand why. A core element of Smith's analysis focuses on the dehumanization aspect of war. As you'll see, this element of war speaks strongly to themes that emerge from evolutionary psychology.

Based on Smith's (2007) analysis, warfare is difficult for people. That is, people are actually disgusted by the idea of killing others—and this evolutionarily shaped motive is in conflict with motives to commit and win wars for such purposes as resource acquisition and benefiting one's broader group and furthering its goals. So war necessarily leads to conflict—and it turns out that large proportions of soldiers intentionally and knowingly shoot away from their enemy, hoping that others will take on the psychologically disgusting act of killing.

It seems that humans have developed an interesting psychological set of processes to help them get over this barrier to killing. And this includes *dehumanizing the enemy*. In a large-scale analysis of war across history and cultures, Smith (2007) finds that dehumanizing the enemy takes some very common forms— and each of these is highly evolutionarily relevant. Dehumanization in warfare includes:

- Portraying the enemy as a predator (such as a snake or raptor)
- Portraying the enemy as a prey animal (such as rabbit or deer)
- Portraying the enemy as a vector of disease (such as a rat or a tick)

In each of these cases, the portrait is of an animal that people often agree *should* be killed. Snakes are dangerous—they should be killed so they can't kill you or your family. Prey animals are to be killed in the context of hunting—with hunting conducted by all-male coalitions as an important part of our evolutionary heritage. And animals that carry disease (such as rats) are to be exterminated. Painting one's enemy as being one of these kinds of animals is a psychological process that makes the enemy more killable. Again, this is not a pretty aspect of humanity but it is a basic aspect of warfare, and the evolutionary perspective certainly helps us better understand why such dehumanization takes place in the context of war.

THE ROCK-THROWING APE

In a significant recent development regarding the ultimate origins of human beings, Paul Bingham and Joanne Souza provide an extraordinary treatise on the importance of projectile weapons in helping shape group coordination and, ultimately, civilization itself in the evolutionary history of our species. Their book, *Death from a Distance and the Birth of a Human Universe*, starts with a single interesting idea that relates importantly to the basic ideas of aggression presented at the start of this chapter. At some point in the evolution of humans, throwing ability became well honed. On first glance, this seems almost like a side note regarding evolutionary history. But this fact has an important implication that relates to the hawks-and-doves analysis. Recall that the hawks-and-doves analysis essentially makes a case for why aggression has high costs on the aggressor. Well, while this point is generally true—conceptually—something happened in human evolution that changed this a bit when it comes to our own species.

Human beings are able to throw objects—such as rocks—with speed and accuracy that are unmatched among primates. Not that we should, but we can kill someone by throwing a rock. So the cost that a person can inflict on another with this simple act is enormous. But what about the cost to oneself? In traditional hand-to-hand fights among humans, things get nasty and bloody for both parties. Even if you can wrestle someone to death (again, not recommended!), you might incur some injuries and pain yourself along the way. But the immediate cost to oneself of killing someone by throwing a rock is small—minimal. For the first time in the history of life, then, Bingham and Souza (2009) argue, a species evolved the capacity to kill conspecifics remotely—from a distance—with nearly no costs to oneself.

To underscore this point, Bingham and Souza (2009) discuss the throwing abilities of closely related primates, such as chimpanzees. Simply, chimpanzees literally cannot throw to save their lives! No other animals can do what we can do when it comes to throwing objects. Compared with a chimp, you're a regular Cy Young award winner! Bet you never thought about that before!

This theory has many important implications for the evolutionary psychology of aggression as well as the evolutionary psychology of human social structures. Regarding aggression, the remote killing capacities of our ancestors allowed individuals to kill or seriously injure others from a distance. This was an entirely new tool in the arsenal of aggression. And one look at the history of warfare shows that the notion of projectile weaponry, which elaborates on this idea of remote killing abilities, clearly took advantage of this aspect of who we are.

In addition to shaping the nature of warfare and weaponry, Bingham and Souza (2009) argue that our remote killing capabilities led to egalitarian social structures and, ultimately, to democracy. In many mammals, one dominant male serves as the leader, has access to most or all the females, and holds a disproportionate amount of power. This fact often corresponds to having a large body and lots of muscles relative to the others. So no one messes with the alpha male because if they do they're going to get hurt!

Think about how remote killing abilities changed this fact in our early human ancestors. While a Hulk-like male is still something to be reckoned with in a wrestling match to the death, five medium-sized males with a pile of rocks and a plan can easily take that hulking alpha male out. Thus, remote killing abilities leveled the playing field. And this fact likely led to multiple outcomes that have come to typify human psychology and social structures. One dominant nasty leader can now have his power stripped by a group of intelligent, modest-sized individuals. It's not too hard to see how this fact could have led to relatively egalitarian social structures. Further, we can even easily see the roots of democracy as a result.

The facts associated with remote killing capacities also would have selected for strong cooperation tendencies, as cooperation combined with remote killing capabilities create an extraordinarily powerful synthesis. Further, we can see how all this would have selected for intelligence over brawn. Being able to organize a group of individuals and design an effective plan to conspire against an unfair and powerful leader takes smarts more than biceps. And this may well be why intelligence and the ability to lead groups are every bit as attractive in our species as is a well-cut body with a clearly delineated six-pack.

SUMMARY: HUMAN NASTINESS REVISITED

Aggression is complex when examined from an evolutionary perspective. All-out aggression toward conspecifics is not generally an effective strategy, and game theory analyses, which examine the costs and benefits of aggressive behavior, hold the key to understanding optimal levels of aggression found in different species. If too much aggression leads to too many costs for the aggression, then aggressive behavior would not be too strongly selected.

Aggression in our species seems to relate importantly to issues of sexual selection with males engaging in more intrasexual physical aggression compared with females—often, as is true in many animal species, with the outcome of aggression relating to access to females. Murder and homicide, ugly as they are, are somewhat typical features of humans, and they seem to have been selected to benefit individuals by taking out intrasexual competitors.

Large-scale aggression leads to warfare, which also seems like a human universal. Warfare seems rooted in our evolutionary heritage, with victories in war leading to access to resources with evolutionary benefits.

War often includes projectile weapons, which speaks to the importance of remote killing capacity in our species. In a recent theoretical development in evolutionary psychology, Bingham and Souza (2009) argue that remote killing abilities actually led to many aspects of our unique humanity, including large-scale cooperation, egalitarianism, and an emphasis on intelligence and effective social abilities.

DISCUSSION/ESSAY EXERCISES

- Describe the idea of *game theory* and how an analysis of "hawk versus dove" strategies can help us understand the evolution of aggressive behavior. Make sure to include a discussion of costs and benefits of aggressive acts in your answer.

- Explain the existence of male physical aggression in terms of intrasexual selection/competition. In your discussion, be sure to discuss the relevance of sexual dimorphism. Finally, address how, according to Buss (2005), homicide and murder may be thought to have adaptive benefits and may be related to intrasexual competition.
- Describe David Livingstone Smith's (2008) evolutionarily informed theory of war. In your answer, explain what Smith means by the idea the people are both fascinated and repulsed by war. Finally, describe three specific evolutionarily informed mechanisms of dehumanization that Smith raises as it relates to human warfare.
- Briefly describe how Bingham and Souza's (2009) idea of low costs associated with killing abilities in our hominid ancestors is key in helping understand human uniqueness. In your answer, address how their theory accounts for the democratization of humans as it relates to stone-throwing ability.

Applied Evolutionary Psychology and the Future of the Field

y this point in the book, you realize that evolutionary psychology has implications for all aspects of what it means to be human. In this section, we talk about implications of evolutionary psychology and applications of this way of thinking to problems across humanity writ large. Implications for addressing social problems, such as racism, poverty, and poor education, are discussed with an eye toward seeing how evolutionary psychology can shed light on these important issues.

Further, this section addresses controversies that have surrounded evolutionary psychology. This field has been surrounded by controversy since its inception. Critics of the field often accuse it of being sexist, racist, and overly genetically deterministic—implying that the very intellectual approach of evolutionary psychology is somehow pernicious and evil. The nature of these criticisms will be presented, along with reasoned arguments for the other side. The goal of this chapter is to openly present the relevant issues while concurrently moving toward a concilia-tory resolution, which suggests that people should remain criti-cal of many aspects of evolutionary psychology—as they should remain critical of any intellectual approach to human behavior—but that they keep an open mind as well regarding its power to shed light on who we are.

Finally, to wrap the book up with an eye toward the future, this section addresses potential futures for the field. As my col-leagues and I wrote in a recent article published in the journal *Futures* (Garcia et al., 2011), the future of evolutionary psychology is unclear. As the most interdisciplinary and, perhaps, powerful paradigmatic approach within the behavioral sciences, this area of inquiry has potential to connect all areas of human inquiry, including sociology, psychology, anthropology, literary studies, and more. On the other hand, resistance to the field is down-right palpable—and this resistance does not seem to be letting up. As such, the future of evolutionary psychology is necessarily uncertain. The final chapter summarizes the relevant issues and discusses different factors that will affect the future of evolution-ary psychology.

Evolutionary Psychology Applied to Issues of Humanity

KEY TERMS

- Art conceptualized as a courtship display
- Small- versus large-scale politics
- Coercive threat and politics
- Figueredo et al.'s (2008) ideas on psychopaths and cities
- Issues of urban planning from an evolutionary perspective
- The Binghamton Neighborhood Project
- Social capital
- Pregnancy sickness from an evolutionary perspective
- *Paleo* exercise and diet
- The Applied Evolutionary Psychology Society (AEPS)
- Evolutionary mismatch and psychological disorders
- Mutation-by-selection balance and mental disorders

volutionary psychology fully embraces an approach that sees evolution as relevant to all aspects of the human experience. To this point, we've seen evolutionary psychology applied to such important domains as child development, educational systems, social relationships, understanding family, understanding intimate relationships, understanding sex, understanding infidelity, understanding altruism and aggression, and more. As you can see, evolutionary psychology relates to all important facets of human behavior.

With this in mind, forward-thinking citizens—as we are (I'm guessing!)—might be wise to apply evolutionary psychology to the many problems and issues that surround human existence. While I believe that the application of evolutionary psychology to helping us solve problems is extremely untapped, in this chapter I present research on several applied areas that have been elucidated by applications of evolutionary psychology.

In any science, there is a distinction between *basic* and *applied* research. Basic research is designed to help us understand and learn more about a phenomenon without a specific eye toward application. For instance, research on the evolutionary psychology of preferences in potential mates conducted by David Buss and his colleagues (1989) has been useful in helping us understand human mating, but this research was not conducted to explicitly help solve any particular problems. That's a characteristic of basic research. In this chapter, we explore applied research—research that is partly conducted to answer certain questions but primarily conducted to be applied to a specific problem.

THE APPLIED EVOLUTIONARY PSYCHOLOGY SOCIETY

In recent years, much excitement among evolutionary psychologists has revolved around the idea of evolutionary psychology applied to help address various personal and societal issues. This work is manifest in the recent creation of the Applied Evolutionary Psychology Society (AEPS), which is dedicated to furthering our knowledge of how evolutionary psychology can be applied to help make the world a better place. Being created on the shoulders of such greats as Alice Andrews, Nick Armenti, Daniel Glass, Daniel Kruger, Daniel O'Brien, and Nando Pelusi (among several others), this initiative holds the following mission from aepsociety.org):

> The mission of the Applied Evolutionary Psychology Society (AEPS) is to promote the use of evolutionary theory in applied fields such as policy making, business, law, education, medicine, and mental health. To achieve this goal, AEPS holds academic workshops and conferences to provide resources for, and connections between, researchers on the one hand, and practitioners, policy makers, executives, and the general public on the other.
>
> The theoretical and empirical findings that have emerged from evolutionary psychology over the past several decades have laid the foundation for a novel approach to solving the vast array of social, political, and ecological challenges we now face. Indeed, the insights that the human evolutionary sciences have provided have important consequences for establishing and generating evolutionarily informed (EI) and EI-applied solutions to our social and environmental problems. AEPS evolved to support evolutionists in translating their findings into practical applications and is dedicated to the development and dissemination of the prosocial applications of evolutionary theory.
>
> Several evolutionary scientists have already addressed a number of these issues from an EI perspective. David Sloan Wilson and his colleagues, for example, have applied evolutionary principles to guide their "Binghamton Neighborhood Project" with the goal that "the BNP can become a model of community-based research informed by modern scientific theory and methods." We seek more of that; more evolutionarily-informed problem-solving procedures such as EI parenting; EI environmental conservation; EI psychotherapy; EI medicine; EI education; EI nutrition and exercise programs; EI business procedures; EI

public-policy making; and more. AEPS can serve as a clearing-house for proposed evolutionary psychological practical solutions to problems in living.

This mission captures the basic ideas of applied evolutionary psychology quite well. And, as an added benefit, the acronym for the society, AEPS, is pronounced "apes!" (yes, this was by design!).

With all this in mind, we can see that applied evolutionary psychology is extremely broad in its potential scope. In this chapter, we examine several specific aspects of applied evolutionary psychology to provide a sampling of this exciting new area of academic inquiry.

THE AESTHETIC APE: EVOLUTIONARY PSYCHOLOGY APPLIED TO THE ARTS

Evolutionary psychologists are particularly interested in areas of functioning that are accurately described as human universals. And when it comes to the arts, there are many such universals. While artistic products are notorious for varying dramatically across cultures (modern rap music in North America is pretty different from opera music from the 19th century in Europe), that such art forms exist across such varied groups of people speaks to the fact that there's something basic about the need to express the thoughts and feelings of individuals by using the same basic kinds of art forms. In short, the music sounds quite different across two cultures, but it's noteworthy that both cultures have music!

Several major scholarly efforts in the past few years have investigated various art forms from an evolutionary perspective. The scholars behind this work include Dennis Dutton (*The Art Instinct*, 2010), Geoffrey Miller (*The Mating Mind*, 2000), and Steven Pinker (*The Blank Slate*, 2003). While these scholars don't fully agree with one another on the details, they all agree that art is a basic aspect of human evolved psychology and that ideas from evolutionary psychology play a significant role in helping us understand the ultimate reasons for art.

Dutton and Miller largely take a fitness-indicator approach to art, seeing art forms as mechanisms by which individuals display their quality, and these displays are often used in courtship contexts. This angle largely focuses on the fact that art is attractive and hard to fake, so it's an honest signal of one's quality—perhaps even one's genetic quality.

In a study on the fitness-indicator model of art, Haselton and Miller (2006) asked a large sample of women if they were more attracted to (a) an artist who was of low quality but who happened to get lucky and made a lot of money from his art, versus (b) an artist who was objectively outstanding at his craft, but who was (like many artists) poor when it comes to money. These researchers also asked questions to tap where the women were in their ovulatory cycle, and what they found speaks strongly to the fitness-indicator theory of art. Women who were not near their ovulatory peak preferred the bad artist with the money. Women who were near their ovulatory peak, on the other hand, preferred the poor but artistically talented artist. These researchers interpret these data in terms of a fitness-optimization approach, with the idea that high-quality art is a window into a high-quality nervous system and, thus, a high-quality set of DNA. And when better to unconsciously focus on selecting a high-quality mate than when one is actually capable of conceiving?

This perspective of art as having evolved for fitness-indicator purposes also is evidenced by the famous sexual histories of so many successful artists—think Jimi Hendrix or Jim Morrison, whose extensive sexual histories are as legendary as their premature and controversial deaths.

This take on art helps us understand a major piece of the humanity puzzle. So much scholarship goes into understanding art, teaching students skills to create art, understanding the history of art, and so on. Art is a huge part of who we are, but it, almost by definition, has no survival value, which is probably

why art programs are often the first to be cut when school bud-
get axes come around each year. The fitness-indicator perspective
gives a sense of *why* art exists and how basic it is to the formation
and maintenance of human social relationships.

Further approaches to the evolutionary psychology of art
focus on the content of art, which often tells a story of universal-
ity in themes that emerge across varied aspects of art. For instance,
in an analysis of song lyrics from different genres, Hobbs and
Gallup (2011) found that themes related to sexual selection
emerge in spades. And this work is consistent with the idea of
art forms as serving sexual display functions. Finally, Pinker
(2002) points out that many themes emerge and reemerge in
the visual arts—including bodies of beautiful people, landscapes
that include fitness-affording entities such as water or food, and
other qualities that we find pleasing largely because these qualities match aspects of ancestral environments that related to fitness-enhancing outcomes.

EVOLUTIONARY PSYCHOLOGY
AND POLITICS

The older you get, the more you come to see that politics are
prominent features of any and all social context—life is filled
with politics at all levels, and the evolutionary perspective helps
us understand this fact. Further, an evolutionary perspective
helps us understand the kinds of issues that ultimately underlie
politics in humans.

In the newest research project that I'm conducting with
the New Paltz Evolutionary Psychology Lab, we're examining
the nature of different kinds of politics as they relate to human
psychology. Our basic prediction is that immediate, local politics related to one's social or familial circle will be more psychologically accessible and affecting compared with the kinds
of large-scale politics that we typically think of. For instance,

we're predicting that a person will be more distressed—and have more to say about—a situation in which a nasty colleague got a $4,000-a-year raise instead of himself or herself compared to a situation in which the current president and Congress passed a bill that raises one's taxes by this same amount a year. The idea here is that in the environment of evolutionary adaptedness, there was no such thing as large-scale, nonlocal politics, so our minds are likely much better able to effectively process issues of local politics. This research is ongoing, but it seems that our prediction is likely to be supported. These findings may have important implications for our understanding of large-scale politics—namely, if we can document that people generally misunderstand or de-emphasize large-scale politics, then we have a better understanding of some of the political-apathy issues that we often see. Further, this research might suggest that getting people to care about large-scale politics may benefit from having large-scale political issues framed in small-scale kinds of ways.

In their groundbreaking work on the importance of projectile weapons in shaping the evolution of human psychology, Bingham and Souza (2009) demarcate several important implications regarding politics from an evolutionary perspective. In this work, featured in a special issue of the *Journal of Social, Evolutionary, and Cultural Psychology* dedicated to applications of evolutionary psychology, Bingham and Souza (2012) use their novel theory of how coercive threat that follows from the remote killing abilities that our ancestors evolved has important implications for our understanding of large-scale politics. Specifically, they write, "Evolutionary psychology has made enormous progress in understanding how individual and kin selection shape our sexual and family behaviors. In striking contrast, our understanding of the evolution of our uniquely massive scale of social cooperation (kinship-independent; subjectively, the 'public' sphere) has been seriously incomplete" (p. 360).

Since the rise of civilization after the advent of agriculture 10,000 years ago, the size of human groups has grown at breakneck speed (by evolutionary standards). Large cities now can include more than 10,000,000 individuals—a far cry from Dunbar's number of 150, which represents the number of people that our minds are familiar with in a social group based on the size of groups in our ancestral past. As Bingham and Souza (2012) point out, new weapon-related technologies across human history have consistently led to an expansion of the size of human groups. This finding is based on the idea that as projectile weapons became more advanced, smaller groups were able, through coercive threat, to control larger and larger groups of humans. Once guns were created and distributed to armies, these armies could exert a larger influence on people they were trying to control. Thus, others had important motivations to join the side of the group with the more advanced weapons. And this ends up being a major theme of the expansion of human groups.

But our social minds are simply not prepared for dealing with such large groups, making large-scale politics tricky for creatures like us. Thinking about a war in a far-off place that has no direct effects on one's own immediate lot is simply evolutionarily unnatural. For modern politicians to be effective, they need to create and implement public policies in a way that takes this fact of our evolved psychology into account and that therefore facilitates our thinking about large-scale politics in a small-scale manner.

EVOLUTIONARY PSYCHOLOGY AND THE STRUCTURE OF CITIES

A related line of modern applied evolutionary psychology pertains to the nature of cities. Cities are large and, as you can see by a common theme in this chapter, they are in many ways evolutionarily unnatural, simply based on sheer numbers. In a provocative comment on modern ecological conditions that mismatch ancestral conditions, Figueredo, Brumbach, Jones, Sefcek, Vasquez, and Jacobs (2008) suggest that cities provide a niche for individuals who have a heritable tendency toward psychopathy, or the tendency to exploit others and utilize others for their own purposes without caring about the feelings or outcomes of others. The reasoning here is that under ancestral conditions, individuals with strong psychopathic tendencies would have not stood much of a chance. The rumor mill in a group of 150 was small, and psychopathic, exploitive behavior would simply have not been able to be hidden from other members of one's group.

In a large city, the door is, actually, wide open for psychopathic tendencies. If you wanted to, you could exploit a new person whom you'd probably never see again each day in a city as large as Toronto or Los Angeles, for instance. Yes, this is a scary thought and it speaks to some of the psychological liabilities that come with the "advancement of civilization." Putting humans in a large city leads to many instances of evolutionary mismatch. Modern evolutionary psychology helps us understand points of mismatch and, as such, this perspective may well help us design and run modern communities—cities included—in a way that benefits from our understanding of the evolutionary origins of the human mind.

In a specific line of work based on this kind of reasoning, David Sloan Wilson and his students have taken this reasoning to heart. Specifically, they have conducted a large-scale research project on their home city of Binghamton, New York, in an effort to improve the quality of life for people by implementing applied evolutionary psychology. Summarized in his book *The Neighborhood Project*, Wilson's (2011) project started premised on the fact that Binghamton is a struggling city. Once a booming city that boasted rights to the inception of IBM, the city has fallen upon difficult economic times in the past several decades with increases in crime and substance abuse—things that go hand-in-hand with difficult economic times.

So how would an evolutionist go about trying to address these kinds of urban problems? In short, Wilson thought about this project as a behavioral ecologist—someone who studies an organism's life in relation to its environment—with an eye toward mismatches between current and ancestral (environment of evolutionary adaptedness-based) conditions. After collecting broad-based psychological data on hundreds of students in the city's school system, a first step in this project was to examine the nature of neighborhoods that corresponded to students who are doing well academically and socially, as well as an assessment of the nature of neighborhoods that correspond to students who are having problems academically and socially.

Beyond the effects of socioeconomic status, Wilson found strong evidence for the importance of neighborhood variability in *social capital*. By this he essentially means neighborhoods that show signs of connectedness among the people in the neighborhood—Jack-o-lanterns in October, Christmas lights, Easter eggs hanging from maple trees, and so forth, were assessed initially as easy-to-operationalize starting variables. Even among the poor areas, children who come from neighborhoods that score high on social capital tend to perform better at school than children from other neighborhoods, and they score higher on indices of natural altruistic tendencies.

In large cities, there are microsystems—neighborhoods. While a city of several hundred thousand can't possibly replicate the ecological details of social groups in the environment of evolutionary adaptedness, a neighborhood, appropriately sized and appropriately structured, just might be able to come close. And this vision, informed by evolutionary psychology, may help us radically rethink the nature of urban planning and maintenance. Wilson's *Neighborhood Project* sits as a significant step along these lines.

EVOLUTIONARY PSYCHOLOGY AND PHYSICAL HEALTH

In a recent landmark trend that integrates the juggernaut industries of higher education and health, evolutionary approaches to human health have come to emerge high on the radar of many.

And evolutionary psychology, in particular, is playing a major role in this movement.

Sometimes referred to as *evolutionary medicine* or as *paleo approaches to health*, modern medicine has finally started to take evolution seriously. This point may sound strange, as medical professionals are essentially applied biologists—and you'd think "how could they *not* be evolutionist in their approach?"— but, as it turns out, modern medicine has progressed for years without any serious consideration of human evolutionary origins.

For instance, for decades, pregnant women who experienced *morning sickness* or *pregnancy sickness* were treated with medications designed to address the symptoms. Nausea is not good, and reducing the nausea seemed like a reasonable prescription. However, it turns out that until 1992, no one in the medical community had ever thought about the evolutionary origins regarding *why* pregnancy sickness exists. What is its evolutionary function? Unfortunately, as a result of this major oversight, pharmaceutical treatments for pregnancy sickness, for years led to adverse developmental physical outcomes in many developing fetuses in the modern world.

In a landmark paper on the topic of pregnancy sickness from an evolutionary perspective, evolutionary psychologist Marge Profet (1992) examined several sources of evidence that speak to the adaptive evolutionary function of pregnancy sickness. Using multiple sources of convergent evidence that characterize the best of research in evolutionary psychology (see Schmitt & Pilcher, 2004), Profet documented the following:

- Pregnancy sickness is found across the globe—it is a human universal.
- Pregnancy sickness is often a response to vegetables and other foods with low levels of toxins that are not dangerous to a pregnant mother but that may be dangerous to a developing fetus.

● Pregnancy sickness tends to characterize pregnancies during precisely the time that the major organs are developing.

In fact, Profet (1992) uncovered several other factors that underlie pregnancy sickness, but the short list presented here provides enough for you to see the adaptive roots of this phenomenon. Being sick and throwing up foods that may lead to adverse consequences for a developing fetus is, simply, very reasonably conceptualized as an adaptation. It's a form of natural medication.

In fact, evolutionary approaches to medicine often have this same bottom line; that is, the idea that there are natural ways to address health issues. In particular, this approach focuses on qualities of ancestral environments that related to health outcomes—and how we can use this understanding to help inform modern medical practices.

Perhaps the hottest areas of work on this topic these days relate to diet and exercise from an evolutionary perspective. With many heavyweight scholars, such as Colorado State's Loren Cordain (2010) and Harvard's Richard Wrangham (2010) working on this topic, and many bright and articulate authors with the ability to make this work accessible, such as Robb Wolf (2011) who wrote *The Paleo Solution*, the current trend toward preagricultural forms of diet and exercise is enormous.

Like any area of inquiry, this field is not without controversies and many of the details are being worked out by researchers across the globe. But this said, the evolutionary perspective, in general, and the idea of evolutionary mismatch, in particular, can provide us with a major framework for understanding so many health issues that permeate modern societies.

Premised on the idea of evolutionary mismatch, the basic reasoning is this: In thinking about what kind of exercise we should do or what we should eat, we need to strongly consider what things were like before agriculture. Our minds and bodies evolved primarily under preagricultural conditions, and things have changed in our environments dramatically since then. Perhaps the optimal diets and exercise regimens for humans can be found in our understanding of the environments and habits of our preagrarian ancestors.

This idea makes sense largely in terms of an ironic detail of modern human health. In westernized societies, we have many health problems, such as obesity and type 2 diabetes that are just not common in nonwesternized societies. If we're all that, why are we so fat?

Since the advent of agriculture, people have started eating all kinds of things that did not exist before agriculture. Our ability to process foods has led to the large-scale production of food that helps fend off starvation, but many of these same foods, such as wheat, cow's milk, and their derivatives, are simply unnatural. Cheese, butter, pasta, bread, cake; sure, I like all of these, too—but these are processed foods that only exist in light of very recent agricultural advances. And they partly are so popular because they exploit human evolved food preferences. People like sugary and high-fat foods not because they were common during prehistory, but, rather, because they were uncommon! These kinds of foods—high fat meat or very sugary fruit—were rare. But getting your hands on them under ancestral conditions was to your benefit because of the real threat of famine and drought. If you and your clan were likely to go without food for a month, you better stock up and put some meat on your bones as best as you could! And our evolved food preferences map onto this reasoning.

These foods were rare, so our preferences were shaped such that we would *really* like this stuff to motivate us to eat it—and our ancestors who had these kinds of preferences were more likely to survive famine conditions and come to pass on genes coding for these taste preferences.

Under modern conditions, these same evolved taste preferences, ironically, lead to many health problems. Not enough time since the advent of agriculture has elapsed for these preferences to be "selected out" of the gene pool. So the same preferences that conferred adaptive benefits to our preagrarian ancestors lead to things like obesity and cardiovascular disease in a world filled with McDonald's. In fact, the success of restaurants like McDonald's speaks to our evolved food preferences. Under ancestral conditions, high-fat and high-sugar foods were rare, and obtaining them whenever you could led to health benefits on average. Now, due to advances in modern agriculture and industry, businesses can exploit our ancestral preferences for profit. They can crank out cheeseburgers and milkshakes for low cost all day long. And they do. And they sell billions and billions. And this is an exploitation of a major mismatch between the environment of evolutionary adaptedness and modern environments. Ironically, it's less expensive to eat cheap, processed, unnatural foods than it is to eat the kinds of foods that did exist under the environment of evolutionary adaptedness (meats, fishes, fruits, nuts, berries, and vegetables, for instance). As a result, the poor people in a westernized society have fewer healthy food choices, and "Western diseases" such as type 2 diabetes disproportionately affect people in impoverished conditions. Understanding nutrition from an evolutionary perspective can help.

And the modern trends in paleo-based exercise regimens tell a similar tale. Crossfit and other modern fitness movements are premised on the idea that people have evolved to do certain kinds of exercises and movements. Our ancestors did not sit on couches eating potato chips and watching reality TV shows! Before agriculture, humans were nomadic—they moved. And movement necessitates exercise. Lifting, walking, running, climbing, and so forth.

While much needs to be done to document the long-term benefits of adopting natural, evolutionary-based nutritional and exercise programs, it's clear that understanding our ancestral past and the nature of evolution has enormous implications for optimizing human health (see Platek, Geher, Heywood, Stapell, Porter, & Waters, 2011).

EVOLUTIONARY PSYCHOLOGY AND MENTAL HEALTH

When people think of *psychology*, they often think of abnormal psychological states and therapy. Clearly, a student in an academic psychology program learns quickly that psychology is much bigger than this particular area—including much in the way of basic science, theory, and research regarding all kinds of behavioral phenomena.

This said, the psychology of abnormality and therapy is, in fact, a major area of applied psychology, and many evolutionary psychologists have examined these applied issues.

A basic question addressed by scholars in this area pertains to questions of etiology: Why do psychological abnormal conditions exist? And how can we best understand them? Clearly there are many different classes of psychological abnormality, and different conditions often have different roots. As such, different evolutionary-based explanations have been proposed to understand different clinical phenomena.

A major evolutionary approach to understanding mental disorders pertains to the idea of evolutionary mismatch. Some psychological problems have been framed as being adaptive under ancestral conditions but maladaptive under modern conditions. For instance, bipolar disorder, characterized as oscillating between bright and active manic periods and relatively depressed periods, is a major psychological disorder. One theory of the evolutionary origins of this disorder speaks to the major differences found in the amount of daylight under ancestral conditions across the year. With modern artificial lighting, people take care of business as usual year round. Under ancestral conditions, people, particularly in northern latitudes, dealt with long periods of light during one part of the year and long periods of dark at other times. Differential levels of activity to match this pattern make sense—and this fact of ancestral environments may elucidate the nature of bipolar disorder (Gallup, 2012).

Evolutionary approaches have also helped us better under-stand important distinctions among versions of disorders that have previously been overlooked. For instance, Keller and Nesse (2006) examined the *Diagnostic and Statistical Manual of Mental Disorders* or *DSM* criteria for depression (with *DSM criteria* correspond-ing to guidelines used by the American Psychiatric Association to classify different disorders) and concluded that these criteria are incomplete. The criteria lump together symptoms such as seeking social isolation and rumination. In fact, Keller and Nesse, taking an evolutionary approach, argue that different kinds of situations under ancestral conditions would have led to different reasons for depression. Death of a loved one, for instance, would have led to important pressures on an individual to seek social bonds and con-nections to compensate for an important loss in one's social net-work. On the other hand, a major public failure in some domain, such as failing to emerge in an important leadership position, might lead to shame and reasons to seek isolation, and perhaps to much rumination designed to help one understand where he or she has gone wrong. For these reasons, the symptoms of depres-sion depend importantly on the causes of depression. Depression caused by loss should lead to seeking social support, while depres-sion caused by failure should lead to the exact opposite *symptom*— and this is exactly what Keller and Nesse (2006) found in their research on a large sample of clinically depressed individuals.

Another major theory of psychological disorder from the work of evolutionary psychology pertains to the idea of *mutation-by-selection balance* (Keller & Miller, 2006). This idea pertains to a paradoxical element of psychological disorders. If these disorders lead to poor functioning and are rated as unattractive in potential mates (and some research has verified this point; Keller & Miller [2006]), and they are partly heritable (as they generally are; Keller & Miler [2006]), how is it that disorders such as schizo-phrenia reappear across generations? In a fascinating summary of work on the evolutionary psychology of disorders, Keller and Miller argue that psychological disorders are partly the result of *high mutation load*—or genetic mutations across the genome that result from copying errors in the DNA replication process. This idea would account for why these disorders return across generations. The idea is that they naturally result from copying errors that are inherent in the process of sexual reproduction.

When it comes to understanding psychological disorders from an evolutionary perspective, there are many different angles, such as the idea of evolutionary mismatch, the emphasis on specific ecological conditions that relate to disordered conditions, or the idea of disorders as indicators of mutation load.

With the burgeoning field of evolutionary clinical psychology (see Glass, 2012), it is clear that evolutionary psychology is well positioned to shed light on the nature of psychological disorders—to help the behavioral sciences better understand and address these kinds of issues in the future and to help clinicians and counselors better understand the issues that their clients face—from an ultimate perspective.

SUMMARY: EVOLUTIONARY PSYCHOLOGY CAN SAVE THE WORLD!

Given how relevant evolutionary psychology is to so many aspects of humanity, this field is poised to help us understand many important personal and societal problems. The Applied Evolutionary Psychology Society (AEPS) has recently entered the scene as a major intellectual organization designed to help catalyze applied work in the field of psychology to help shed light on some of the most important issues of humanity.

Toward this end, applied evolutionary psychologists have helped shed light on such issues of the nature of music and art, politics, urban planning, child development and education, medicine, nutrition, exercise, and mental health. To this point, only the tip of the iceberg has been revealed regarding how powerful evolutionary psychology will be in helping us better understand the human condition.

DISCUSSION/ESSAY EXERCISES

● Briefly describe the mission of Applied Evolutionary Psychology Society (AEPS) along with specific areas of inquiry that it is trying to enhance. In your answer, be sure to describe the distinction between "basic" and "applied" research. Finally, describe one specific example (theoretical or documented) of the kind of applied evolutionary psychology that the AEPS tries to foster.

● Describe how sexual selection theory has been used to help us understand the nature of art (Miller, 2000). In your discussion, briefly describe some research addressing specifically how art may be conceptualized as a courtship device.

● Briefly describe the interface of evolution and medicine. In your answer, address different areas of human health that are being elucidated by the application of an evolutionary perspective.

● Describe mental disorders from an evolutionary perspective. In your answer, address some specific disorders that have been studied from an evolutionary perspective along with the specific ideas from evolutionary psychology that have been applied to help elucidate these phenomena.

Controversies Surrounding Evolutionary Psychology

*Evolutionary psychology (is) . . . subject to a level of
implacable hostility which seems far out of proportion
to anything even sober reason or common politeness
might sanction.*

(Dawkins, 2005, p. 975)

KEY TERMS

- Conditional strategism
- Digesting anomalies
- Eugenics
- Evolved behavioral sex differences
- Falsifiability in science
- Genetic determinism

- Human universals
- Nonconditional strategism
- Progressivity in science
- Religious fundamentalism as related to evolutionary psychology
- Schmitt and Pilcher's (2004) work on the role of convergent evidence in evolutionary psychology
- Situationism as related to evolutionary psychology

s a perspective—rather than a content area of psychology—evolutionary psychology is positioned differently than other areas of psychology. We make big claims, and not everyone likes that! Evolutionary psychologists make claims about the ultimate origins of all psychological processes, and we make claims about all sub areas of the behavioral sciences (and beyond). While evolutionary psychologists see this approach as integrative, others seem to find it off-putting.

There are many controversial aspects of evolutionary psychology, and understanding these controversies and voices on different sides of these issues can be very helpful in allowing students to take content away from a course in evolutionary psychology while concurrently having healthy skepticism and an open mind when it comes to the controversies surrounding this field.

As author of this book, I believe I'm actually uniquely positioned to comment on this particular topic. My home institution, SUNY New Paltz, has heard the expression of many voices regarding evolutionary psychology—including several critical perspectives. This feature of our academic environment has been extremely useful for my students and me in understanding the criticisms of this field and helping to forge intellectual bridges with other academic areas. In short, being an evolutionary psychologist at SUNY New Paltz has provided me with a unique window on the controversies that surround this area. This chapter is my attempt to share what I've seen through this window with the readers of this book.

MAJOR CONTROVERSIES SURROUNDING EVOLUTIONARY PSYCHOLOGY

As you'll see, my research has shown that one of the most contentious controversies in evolutionary psychology relates to the idea of evolved behavioral sex differences—the idea that men and women show some natural differences as a result of evolutionary processes. Including this particular issue, controversies that will be addressed in this chapter include the following:

* Evolved behavioral sex differences
* Religion
* Genetic determinism
* Bad science
* Eugenics

The Evolved Behavioral Sex Differences Controversy

In 2006, my good friend and colleague Alice Andrews, who also teaches evolutionary psychology at SUNY New Paltz, asked me to contribute a piece to a unique journal that she edited at the time—*Entelechy*. A vibrant journal in its time, *Entelechy* was dedicated to integrating evolutionary perspectives into the arts, with the goal of creating cross-disciplinary dialogue designed to harness the excitement that evolutionary ideas can bring to the humanities. My contribution was perhaps the most fun article I've ever published. I wrote it at a time when evolutionary psychology's role was being highly contested on my home campus—particularly as it relates to the issue of evolved behavioral sex differences. In this chapter, I present this article to spearhead discussion of the issues at hand.

DO INNATE BEHAVIORAL DIFFERENCES BETWEEN DOGS AND CATS EXIST?[1]

A Debate Between the Esteemed Canine Constructionist Psychologist, Dr. ArfArf Anythinggoes of Sheppard State University and the Renowned Feline Evolutionary Psychologist, Professor MeowMeow Immutable, of Carnivore College

Moderated by Celina the Seemingly Centrist Squirrel

Celina: Thank you all for attending this important debate. Of course, this debate is extremely topical in light of the recent comments of President Pawinmouth of Carnivore College, who suggest that dogs and cats may have different general skills from one another because of innate differences between the species.

Welcome, to our esteemed panelists and guests. Okay, let's get started. Let's start with the heart of the matter . . .

Professor Immutable, evolutionary psychologists are often accused of being specist, assuming that cats are naturally better than dogs, and thus deserve higher status and more power across all elements of our society. How do you respond to such criticism?

Professor MeowMeow Immutable: First, many thanks to Celina for hosting this important debate. Are cats naturally better than dogs? That's like saying that blue is naturally better than red. The evolutionary approach to differences between cats and dogs emphasizes *similarities* between the species to the extent that environmental pressures across their evolutionary heritages were similar, and, further, this perspective predicts phenotypal differences between dogs and cats to the extent that such pressures were *different* across evolutionary time.

Dr. ArfArf Anythinggoes: MeowMeow—think about the societal implications of this doctrine! While your ostensibly scientific account of predicted differences between the species seems reasonable, it neglects the important social ramifications that are implied! If we accept that cats are presumably naturally "different" from dogs, then we are essentially endorsing a dangerous philosophy of "separate but equal." It is our obligation as citizens to work against such a way of thinking.

Professor MeowMeow Immutable: But consider the compelling nature of the evidence supporting the notion of psychological differences between cats and dogs! Across all cultures, dogs are more social than are cats. Further, across all cultures, cats are considerably less able to be trained to jump through hoops and the like compared with dogs. This analysis is not value laden, it is simply fact based.

Dr. ArfArf Anythinggoes: Nonsense! In my 35 years of research on this topic, I have found, time and time again, that any apparent differences between cats and dogs are attributable to social roles, social expectations, and social-constructionist processes. For instance, in my lab, we have consistently documented that cats are capable of jumping through hoops! We've all simply been socialized so as not to *expect* cats to be able to jump through hoops. Worse, this pattern of socialization may have detrimental effects on the self-esteem of cats in general. So you see, my constructionist analysis is just as concerned with the welfare of cats as it is with the welfare of dogs!

Celina: Okay, I think we are getting somewhere. Professor Immutable, your approach is often framed as a genetically deterministic approach. How do you respond to such comments?

Professor MeowMeow Immutable: Celina, that criticism is so off target and misguided! While evolutionary psychologists believe that behavioral patterns of all species evolved via evolutionary forces, we also believe that most organisms show a great deal of behavioral flexibility in light of changes in environmental conditions. For instance, while we would argue that dogs are generally likely to form groups with social rules and such, more so than are cats, we also believe that dogs may be encouraged to be relatively solitary under certain conditions. We hardly believe that each species has one simple, immutable way of being.

Dr. ArfArf Anythinggoes: MeowMeow, I must say that I am uncomfortable with you suggesting that dogs tend to be more "pack oriented" than cats by nature. This proposition is exactly the kind of specist garbage that is poisoning the minds of college students across the country! Society simply expects relatively pack-oriented behavior from dogs more so than from cats—my research demonstrates this point strongly! Structures within society—often created by cats in the first place—clearly play the key role in shaping such behavioral patterns.

Professor MeowMeow Immutable: But the pack-oriented nature of dogs exists in ALL SOCIETIES! Do you really believe that this fact is altogether irrelevant? Might it be that societal rules are actually manifestations of evolutionary processes? That is certainly the stance of evolutionary psychology. Societal rules are not random—and they are not unrelated to our evolutionary heritage. Thus, while they play an important role in shaping behavioral patterns, they are not reasonably conceptualized as "distinct from evolutionary explanations."

Celina: Aha—I see. Now we seem to really be getting somewhere. Okay, I have one more question. Do you believe that there is hope in the future for creating harmony between dogs and cats? Dr. Anythinggoes, you're first this time.

 Dr. ArfArf Anythinggoes: Yes, I do believe that peace between cats and dogs is possible. However, it is only possible if we realize that the apparent differences between them are really the effects of inequitable social structures that have been created primarily by cats, who are consistently promoting their own self-interests. Cats need to own up to their role in creating the kind of specist qualities that typify our society. MeowMeow, your brand of psychology, I'm afraid, works quite against that goal, and I believe that universities should not allow it to be taught for the sake of our society.

 Professor MeowMeow Immutable: ArfArf, you really have my dander up now! To say that *all* differences between cats and dogs are socially constructed by self-interested cats across the history of mammals is preposterous. . . . This view just makes me . . . . *RRRREOWWW!!!!.* . . .

Celina: Oh my . . . MeowMeow, please . . . please get off ArfArf's neck . . . oh . . . this is not good . . . well, there you have it folks!

———————

Digesting *Dogs and Cats* . . . As you'll see throughout this chapter, one of the core sets of criticisms regarding evolutionary psychology has focused on its central idea of behavioral sex differences in humans as being the result of evolution. While there are several controversies surrounding evolutionary psychology, perhaps none are as contentious as this particular idea. In fact, research that will be presented later in this chapter suggests that this particular controversy may be *evolutionary psychology controversy sine qua non* (see Geher & Gambacorta, 2010)—a controversy in evolutionary psychology so large as to be unmatched by the other controversies.

The *Dogs and Cats* piece that you just read is my attempt at a satire on this particular controversy. Much of the criticism toward evolutionary psychologists on this issue has come from people who identify as feminists who take important issue with the idea of there being any inherent biological differences between males and females. To be fair, I understand this concern.

Part of the problem pertains to social implications of scientific findings. In terms of social and policy-related ideology, it's central in our society that people are treated equally, regardless of gender. As a socially progressive democrat with a daughter—whom I constantly remind that she can do anything—I'm sympathetic to this concern. Perhaps, though, there comes a point at which the reality of data and political points of view butt heads with one another. I thought it would be interesting to see how this conversation takes place if we think about something apolitical, such as differences between dogs and cats.

Immutable is essentially an evolutionist, taking the perspective that dogs and cats behave differently from one another partly because of different evolutionary histories. We can think of this idea as comparable to the angle of an evolutionary psychologist who studies male/female differences based on the notion that men and women have faced different adaptive hurdles across evolutionary time.

Anythinggoes is a social-constructionist, taking the perspective that any and all behavioral phenomena are the result exclusively of societal expectations and constructions, and are not relevant to any biological factors. Anythinggoes is comparable to some feminist scholars who believe that any and all differences between males and females are fully the result of such social constructionist forces.

With that said, their debate actually sounds quite a bit like the debates/conversations held between evolutionary psychologists and academics who take a social constructionist view. However, that conversation typically revolves around male/female differences—not differences between cats and dogs!

You can see that there's a lot at stake. Immutable is steadfast on sticking with evolutionarily based explanations and arguments, whereas Anythinggoes focuses on the importance of social constructions and political implications.

Celina, the moderator, seems to have lost control of the discussion and ends up having to end the debate prematurely, as Immutable literally goes for Anythinggoes' jugular!

In fact, one of the interesting elements of academic debates pertains to the fact that participants often leave the debate only to bolster their own perspective and to devalue an alternative perspective even more so. That's about how things go in *Dogs and Cats*.

So while several controversies regarding evolutionary psychology exist, the largest controversy seems to revolve around this idea of evolved behavioral sex differences. In one study, to empirically examine this question regarding the prominence of this particular controversy regarding evolutionary psychology in the landscape of higher education, Dan Gambacorta and I (2010)[2] created a survey with several kinds of questions that we disseminated to hundreds of adults. About half the participants were professors at varying institutions, and others were employed in other professions. We also asked participants what academic area they were in (if they were professors), and we asked participants if they had children.

Dependent variables represented whether participants believed that several attributes are primarily the result of biological evolution versus socialization. Variables addressed attitudes about: (a) sex differences in adults, (b) sex differences in children, (c) sex differences in chickens, (d) human universals, and (e) differences between dogs and cats. Using a Likert scale, participants were asked to rate the degree to which they believed items were due to "nature" versus "nurture."

Sample items from these different subscales are below:

1. Attitudes about whether human behavioral sex differences in adults are shaped by biological evolution (nature) versus socialization (nurture).
   - Sample item: *Women are more responsive than men to the cries of infants.*
2. Attitudes about whether human behavioral sex differences in children are shaped by biological evolution (nature) versus socialization (nurture).
   - Sample item: *Girls develop language skills earlier than boys.*
3. Attitudes about whether behavioral sex differences in chickens (between hens and roosters) are shaped by biological evolution (nature) versus socialization (nurture).
   - Sample item: *Roosters seem to prefer copulating with more than one hen, while hens don't seem to mind copulating with a single rooster.*
4. Attitudes about whether human universals that are not related to sex differences are shaped by biological evolution (nature) versus socialization (nurture).
   - Sample item: *Feces and vomit are found to be universally disgusting among humans.*
5. Attitudes about whether behavioral differences between dogs and cats are shaped by biological evolution (nature) versus socialization (nurture).
   - Sample item: *Dogs are more pack oriented than cats.*

In composite, these measures allowed us to examine the degree to which participants believed that these different kinds of phenomena are differentially due to biological or socialization-based causes.

An important caveat to this research is that we were not asking participants to make fine and nuanced distinctions regarding the interactions between "nature" and "nurture"—this is an important point. We chose this methodology to simplify the presentation of the materials for the participants, so the methodology was designed to strike something of a balance on this issue.

The primary independent variables included parental and academic employment status. We studied parental status thinking that the experience of raising children might influence beliefs about innate causes of behavior. Also, given that scholars in the fields of women's studies and sociology tend to be particularly likely to endorse a social constructionist perspective, academic participants were divided into categories of either "sociology or women's studies" or "other."

Academic employment status was independently predictive of the belief that sex differences are the result of "nurture." This effect was even higher among academics that came from sociology or women's studies backgrounds. The effect of academic employment status also corresponded to seeing behavioral differences between roosters and hens as caused by "nurture." Further, parents were more likely than nonparents to endorse "nature" for the sex-difference variables. Beliefs about differences between cats and dogs and beliefs about causes of human universals (that are not tied to sex differences) were not related to these independent variables, suggesting that the political resistance seems largely localized to the idea of evolved behavioral sex differences.

Interestingly, the dependent variable regarding human universals was not related to parental or academic status. In short, this implies that the areas of evolutionary psychology that are aside from issues of male/female differences (e.g., research on the evolutionary psychology of emotions, universal fear responses in humans, etc.) are different in terms of political volatility than are the areas of evolutionary psychology that do relate to male/female differences.

This all provides further evidence that while evolutionary psychology often finds itself surrounded by controversy, the issue of evolved sex differences is, at least within the halls of academia, near the top of this list.

The Religion Controversy

Interestingly, the primary controversy that people often think of when they hear about evolutionary psychology relates to religion. This is likely because evolution and religion have a long history of disagreements going back to Darwin's own internal conflicts on this issue.

As it turns out, conflicts regarding the origins of life, which sit at the heart of most religious concerns regarding evolution, don't tend to emerge in discussions regarding evolutionary psychology. Some fundamentalist Christians will vocally dismiss the field outright, given its connection with evolution writ large, but generally, evolutionary psychologists don't find themselves butting heads with religious fundamentalists.

When it comes to resistance to evolution, people talk about *resistance from the right* and *resistance from the left*, with the former pertaining to conservative, right-wing resistance (often hand-in-hand with religious fundamentalist resistance) and the latter pertaining to resistance from political liberals. To the surprise of many, the resistance from the left tends to be much more palpable in the realm of evolutionary psychology. This is not because people on the left don't "believe in evolution." Rather, social liberalism is often connected with a negative reaction to the idea of innate behavioral qualities, and evolutionary psychology often gets lumped into a group of perspectives that are painted as "genetically deterministic." It is to this issue that we turn next.

The Genetic Determinism Controversy

One reason for the resistance to evolutionary psychology pertains to *genetic determinism* (see Geher, 2006b).[3] This is essentially the idea that people do things because of their genes. Taken to an extreme, this idea implies that only genes matter, and that people actually have no control over their behavior. This is, without question, an inaccurate and dangerous view of human behavior. It's also not consistent with the basic premises of evolutionary psychology, which focus extensively on the impact of situational and contextual factors in shaping the nature of behavior.

One of the beliefs that many people tend to hold about evolutionary psychology is that it is a nonsituational doctrine, suggesting that organisms have just a few immutable, invariant ways of responding that are under the direct control of genes. This portrait of evolutionary psychology is simply inaccurate (see Kurzban & Haselton, 2005). Evolutionary psychology posits that species-typical psychological design features with some heritable component have been shaped by natural and sexual selection. Often, many (but not all) evolutionary psychologists will conceive of such design features as *adaptations*. In any case, such adaptations are rarely understood by evolutionary psychologists as being context independent.

Evolutionary psychologists and biologists make an important distinction between *nonconditional* and *conditional strategies* that describe the phenotypes of different organisms. A classic example of a nonconditional, fully genetically determined (and immutable) strategy is found in male sunfish (Gross, 1982), which come in two varieties. The first variety includes large males who have the ability to acquire sufficient territories in intrasexual competition. The second variety includes smaller, *sneaker* males, who are nearly indiscernible from females and who do not elicit aggressive responses from territory-holding males. While territory-holding males reproduce by honestly attracting females, sneaker males use a somewhat dishonest strategy: they blast their gametes after a female has released her eggs in a large male's territory, thereby using deception as a tool for reproduction. It turns out that the differences between these kinds of males are attributable to genetic differences. As such, the strategies employed are nonconditional.

The notion of *conditional strategies*, on the other hand, corresponds to situations in which an organism modifies its strategy, vis-à-vis variability in situational factors. For instance, male tree frogs (Perrill, Gerhardt, & Daniel, 1978) use strategies similar to male sunfish when it comes to mating. Sometimes, a male will carve out a territory and croak loudly. At other times, a male will hide near a territory-holding male and try to mate with females that are attracted to the croaking, territory-holding male. Importantly, in this species, males have been documented to show *strategic pluralism* (Gangestad & Simpson, 2000); they modify their choice of strategy depending on the nature of such situational factors as the number of male territory holders at a given time.

The use of a variety of strategies by male wood frogs does not suggest that their repertoire of mating behaviors is somehow outside the bounds of natural law, or that these strategies are not designed for the "purpose" of reproduction. Clearly, these mating strategies are related to optimal reproduction, a fact that speaks to their selection by evolutionary processes. As such, evolutionary geneticists (e.g., Maynard Smith, 2002) and evolutionary psychologists (e.g., Gangestad & Simpson, 2000) have come to apply evolutionary reasoning to our understanding of mixed behavioral strategies that are highly context sensitive.

In fact, modern-day evolutionary psychology is an extraordinarily situationist perspective. Consider, for instance, evolutionarily informed research on homicide and familial violence. All of the most highly cited work in this area focus on situational factors that underlie family violence. For instance, Daly and Wilson's (1988) often-cited work on violence toward children is all about contextual factors that covary with this atrocious act. Simply, the presence of a step-parent in a household has been shown to be the primary contextual factor that predicts fatal violence toward children. Another contextual factor that Daly and Wilson document as having a significant relationship with such violence is the age of a given child (another contextual factor). In fact, their research, which is, in this regard, very prototypical of much work in evolutionary psychology overall, is all about contextual factors that underlie behaviors.

Consider, as another example, research on factors that predict promiscuous behavior on the part of women. Evolutionary psychologists have uncovered such important contextual factors as localized sex ratios, ovulation cycles, a woman's age, and the presence of children from prior mateships (see Buss, 2003)—each such contextual factor serving as an important statistical predictor of female promiscuity. In short, evolutionary psychology is, in fact, a highly situationist perspective, generally conceiving of human behavioral strategies as being extremely flexible and as falling within the realm of this general idea of strategic pluralism.

Evolutionary psychology does not conceptualize humans as genetically guided automatons whose conscious decision-making processes are irrelevant or nonexistent. Rather, this perspective sees humans as capable of extraordinary conscious decision making. Further, with its roots in strategic pluralism, evolutionary psychology is situationist at its core. Importantly, evolutionary psychology has lessons to provide regarding the nature of situationism as an epistemological doctrine. While situationism in the social sciences is often framed as conceiving of human behavior under the strong influence of situational influences (both small and large; see Ross & Nisbett, 1991), this generic brand of situationism has generally been framed in a manner that is devoid of any insights into how important psychological design features have been ultimately shaped by evolutionary forces for the purpose of reproduction.

The kind of situationism that characterizes modern-day evolutionary psychology may be thought of as a sort of *evolutionary situationism*. This particular brand of situationism suggests that while human behavior is largely under the control of situational influences, the particular situational factors that should matter most in affecting behavior are ones that bear directly on factors associated with survival and reproductive success. As such, Daly and Wilson (1988) did not document just any factors that underlie familial violence—they specifically uncovered the role of step-parenting, a situational factor with clear and theoretically predictable relevance to issues tied to genetic fitness (from a strictly genetic-fitness perspective, a step-child shares no genes with a step-parent, which is, thus, costly).

Given the tremendous potential for evolutionary psychology to inform the search for contextual factors that underlie human psychological outcomes, this idea of evolutionary situationism has the potential to create extraordinary bridges between traditional social psychology and evolutionary psychology.

The Bad Science Controversy

In a comment on the state of evolutionary psychology within academia, Richard Dawkins (2005), an evolutionary biologist with some sympathies toward evolutionary psychology, suggests that the bar for the quality of science in evolutionary psychology may actually be set too high. From his perspective, he agrees that extraordinary claims should require extraordinary evidence—but he believes that the basic premises of evolutionary psychology do not constitute extraordinary claims. That is, the idea that human behavior is ultimately the result of evolution is not, from his angle, a controversial idea that should require extraordinary proof.

This said, many scholars have raised issues with the science element of evolutionary psychology. Perhaps most notably, philosopher of science David Buller (2005) presented a critique of evolutionary psychology that addresses both the theoretical underpinnings and several methodological points pertaining to research in this area.

A major element of his critique pertains to what has been called a "just-so story," or the idea that evolutionary psychologists will often take any finding and mold it into an evolutionary explanation in an after-the-fact (posthoc) manner. This accusation is important and is something that we need to strongly consider.

As evolutionary psychologists, we are unable to conduct experimental research going deeply back in time and changing the course of human evolution to test the effects of certain variables. In fact, to make inferences regarding the evolutionary underpinnings of behavior, we must rely on our understanding of the principles of evolution and existing research to help us explain what we are studying. To be honest, sometimes evolutionary psychologists may well overstep the boundaries, finding something simple that fits with an evolutionary explanation and weaving together a just-so story. Importantly, this is likely not intentional, and critics such as Buller are helpful in keeping us honest.

How can we address the just-so story critique? For one, if we are making inferences about human universals (as evolutionary psychologists often are), then we should collect data in a way that best captures this point. As Schmitt and Pilcher (2004) indicate, the better we can collect data on a single topic, the better positioned we are to make claims about such evolutionary concepts as adaptations. For Schmitt and Pilcher (2004), collecting data from samples of multiple cultures and multiple modes (e.g., self-reported data along with physiological data) goes a long way toward helping us make evolution-based inferences.

Critics such as Buller (2005) will often also critique our theoretical approaches, sometimes calling evolutionary psychology, in the terms of the great philosopher Karl Popper (1984), *unfalsifiable*. That is, some point out that regardless of the study outcome, evolutionary psychologists may have a tendency to essentially say, "Yup—that makes sense from an evolutionary perspective!" This criticism essentially suggests that we overapply evolutionary principles and explanations, and that we don't have any safeguards against such overapplication.

Perhaps the most powerful response to these kinds of claims, for me, anyway, comes from Ketelaar and Ellis (2000), who argue that an area of scientific inquiry shouldn't be judged by whether it is falsifiable. Rather, it should be judged primarily by how *progressive* it is and how able that field is to *digest anomalies*. In this context, progressivity refers to the ability to generate novel research questions and, accordingly, the ability to provide new answers and new information about the world that would not be known otherwise. In fact, evolutionary psychology is famous for this kind of work. Research topics such as the influence of step-parenting on family violence (Daly & Wilson, 1988), the evolutionary function of infantile crying and other attachment behaviors (Bowlby, 1969), and the universal nature of human emotion expression (Ekman & Friesen, 1968) all are topics that have been enormously illuminated by an evolutionary approach to behavior. In fact, without an evolutionary framework to guide this research, these topics would remain poorly understood to this day.

Evolutionary psychology, in a similar vein, has shown the ability to guide research that digests anomalies. Before Daly and Wilson (1988) applied an evolutionary framework to understanding the role of being a step-parent in family violence, the effect of being a step-parent on violence was poorly understood and didn't fit in with then-existing theories of violence. This phenomenon was an anomaly. It was the evolutionarily informed work of Daly and Wilson that digested this anomaly—and more.

While the issues of falsifiability and "just-so stories" are valid, raising these matters to the consciousness of evolutionary psychologists has important potential to help strengthen our science. So my comment to the critics is this—keep it up—and thank you!

The Eugenics Controversy

An atypical, ardently negative criticism of evolutionary psychology that I have become aware of (from several of my students) suggests that evolutionary psychology is, in fact, a form of eugenics. As I argue in this section, evolutionary psychology is absolutely not synonymous with eugenics. Period. Eugenics is all about how human societies *should* selectively breed people so that only relatively fit individuals are the ones to reproduce. The goal of eugenism is to create an optimal species. What a disturbing idea this eugenics is! Further, how far from evolutionary psychology it is! Consider, for instance, male sexual jealousy (Daly, Wilson, & Weghorst, 1982)—the tendency, documented across cultures, for males to be particularly upset by thoughts of their female romantic partners engaging in sexual infidelity, coupled with a proclivity toward committing relatively aggressive acts of violence tied to sexual infidelity (relative to females). Evolutionary psychology is interested in how this phenomenon may be species typical and how it may have been shaped by natural selection. Further, evolutionary psychologists are interested in understanding the detrimental impact of this phenomenon on society and are interested, further, in using knowledge gleaned from evolutionarily guided research to help solve social problems associated with this phenomenon.

On the other hand, someone adopting a eugenics perspective would be focusing on improving the species in terms of optimizing the gene pool. Thus, a eugenicist would see such jealousy as bad insofar as it may work to preclude the most fit among us from having more mates than others!

An evolutionary psychologist is focusing on human behavior as shaped to optimize individuals' own chances of reproduction. Evolutionary psychology is (generally) a non–group-selectionist approach to understanding behavior. It very much focuses on behavior as largely serving the purpose of getting one's own genes into the future—with essentially no regard for "saving the species." A eugenicist, on the other hand, believes that we *should* use our understanding of the effects of genes on behavior and bodies to consciously choose who should reproduce and who should not for the good of the species. This perspective suggests that we should optimize the gene pool of the species via selective breeding; that is the goal of eugenics. That is not at all the goal of evolutionary psychology.

From the perspective of eugenics, we should all work to have people like Arnold Schwarzenegger and Britney Spears do all the mating for our species. From the perspective of evolutionary psychology, people were shaped by natural selection to endorse nothing of the kind—rather, from this perspective, we were shaped to work to reproduce our own particular genes, regardless, in fact, of whether we believe ours may actually be the best in the pool! As is delineated in Table 9.1, evolutionary psychology and eugenics differ in:

a. *The level of selection* (for evolutionary psychology, selection happens at the level of the individual, whereas eugenics is generally a group-selectionist idea)

TABLE 9.1 DISTINGUISHING EVOLUTIONARY PSYCHOLOGY FROM EUGENICS

	Evolutionary Psychology	Eugenics
Level of Selection	Natural selection happens at the level of the individual organism. Psychological qualities viewed as "adaptations" are qualities that confer survival and/or reproductive benefits to the organisms possessing the particular qualities.	In large part, eugenics is a group-selectionist doctrine. It suggests that people should work together in selectively breeding humans to make it so that the species will benefit in the future.
	The entity that is presumably "benefiting" here is the individual.	The entity that is presumably "benefiting" here is the species.
The Selector	The process of natural selection (and, perhaps, other evolutionary processes such as sexual selection). Natural selection is a blind process with no intention and no plan.	Individuals or groups of individuals with particular intentional plans/objectives and, often, particular political agendas.
	The selector here is a natural process fully devoid of human intentions and political agendas.	The selector here is a fully human entity, replete with intentions and political agendas.
Basic Goal	Evolutionary psychology represents a basic scientific endeavor. The goal is to use current understanding of evolutionary principles so as to optimize the ability to understand human behavior and psychological processes.	The goal of eugenics is quite applied in nature. The point of this perspective is to apply our understanding of genes to a program of selective breeding of humans.
	This basic scientific paradigm does not have a specific political agenda; increasing understanding of human psychology is the agenda.	This applied perspective has a very specific agenda.

Consciousness	Evolutionary psychologists study many psychological processes that are unconscious in nature. For instance, Cosmides and Tooby (1992) argue that we differentially apply rules of logic, unknowingly, when we are faced with highly evolutionarily relevant versus relatively evolutionarily nonrelevant judgments. Such unconscious processes were shaped by natural selection to serve the purposes of individual reproduction.	The basic idea of eugenics is a highly conscious one. There is not a focus on unconscious psychological processes. Rather, from this perspective, there is a clear and highly conscious plan. The plan is for members of society to selectively breed in a way that would lead to an optimized gene pool for the society at large in the future.
Thoughts on Arnold Schwarzenegger	From the perspective of evolutionary psychology, this man has been endowed with highly adaptive genes. Good for him. Evolutionary psychologists do not want (consciously or not) him to out-reproduce them. Heterosexual male evolutionary psychologists involved in monogamous relationships would not prefer that their female partners would mate with Arnold rather than with themselves.	A eugenicist might see Arnold as a horse breeder would see a blue-ribbon stallion: He should be used as a stud and should be encouraged, from this perspective, to mate with as many (relatively fit) females as possible in hopes of improving the species.

b. *The selector* (for evolutionary psychology, the selector of heritable qualities is blind natural selection; for eugenics, the selector is a group of humans with conscious intent)

c. *Their basic goals* (the goal of an evolutionary psychologist is to use insights gleaned from evolutionary theory to understand human behavior; the basic goal of eugenics is to improve the human gene pool for the purposes of some small, powerful group)

In addition to Table 9.1, which delineates the important distinctions between evolutionary psychology and eugenics, I have provided an example of a multiple-choice test question that further addresses this distinction (see Table 9.2).

TABLE 9.2 **A MULTIPLE-CHOICE EXAMINATION ITEM DEMONSTRATING THE BASIC DISTINCTION BETWEEN EVOLUTIONARY PSYCHOLOGY AND EUGENICS**

From the perspective of evolutionary psychology, psychological characteristics _____ with the primary function of increasing the likelihood that the _____.

A. are selected by natural selection; species in which the adaptation exists will not go extinct

B. should be selectively bred by people; broad group of organisms to which individuals belong (e.g., animals versus plants) will likely out-compete other broad groups of organisms

C. are selected by natural selection; specific individuals displaying such characteristics in ancestral contexts were particularly likely to out-compete conspecifics (i.e., other humans) and thereby reproduce in relatively higher frequencies

D. should be selectively bred by people; fittest members of the species are most likely to survive and reproduce

The correct answer here is C. Evolutionary psychologists focus on qualities that are "adaptive" from the perspective of individuals. However, if the question started with the phrase, "From the perspective of eugenics . . .," the answer would be D.

(The phrase before the semicolon corresponds to the first blank in question; the phrase after the semicolon corresponds to the second blank.)

In thinking about eugenics, a reader might be thinking about who might be a modern-day eugenicist. While I am clearly arguing that anyone looking to evolutionary psychology for hints of eugenics is barking up the wrong tree (so to speak), there are clearly eugenicist implications found in many modern social movements. Given the historical atrocities associated with eugenics and the potential misuse of modern technologies, I think it is very much worth our time to consider current technological, social, and intellectual trends that may ultimately provide a basis for future eugenicist endeavors.

One strikingly large such social movement concerns observations in sperm-donation trends. In sperm donation, women are able to choose qualities of their offspring based on phenotypal features of genetic fathers who have donated sperm. Consider an article published in the *New York Times* (Egan, 2006) dealing with the prevalence of women choosing to have children via sperm donation with no paternal care to assist in the parenting process. According to this article, "The California Cryobank, the largest sperm bank in the country, owed a third of its business to single women in 2005, shipping them 9,600 vials of sperm, each good for one insemination."

In addition to the relatively large economic niche that sperm donation is filling in industrialized societies, this *New York Times* article addresses the nature of the donors who are selected as fathers. The results presented in this article are eye opening. For instance, Egan writes that, "Short donors don't exist; because most women seek out tall ones, most banks don't accept men under 5-foot-9." Further, the article goes on to describe a woman who chose sperm from a tall German rugby player (whom the mother in question describes as "Aryan"). One could argue that the mothers who are choosing sperm in this way are engaging in eugenicist practices. In fact, the parallels between sperm choice and eugenics are made quite explicitly by this allusion to the "Aryan" sperm donor.

This line of thought, interestingly, extends to all nonrandom mate-choice processes in any sexually reproducing species (see Miller, 2000). Once individuals within a species are using criteria to selectively choose to mate with individuals based on the presence of certain phenotypal qualities, parallels regarding eugenics may become apparent. In writing on this topic, Miller writes that "finding mates with good genes is one of the major functions of mate choice (across all sexually reproducing species)" (p. 431). He further writes that

> We could outlaw genetic screening for heritable traits, but I imagine that our jails would have difficulty housing all of the sexually reproducing animals in the world that exercise mate choice—the female humpback whales alone would require prohibitively costly, high-security aquariums.

My point in describing the parallels among the sperm-donation industry, mate choice in general, and eugenics is not to sound alarm bells. (Although this analysis does raise concerns that should be addressed!) Rather, my point here is that there are existing practices in all societies that do potentially have some eugenicist overtones. Further, importantly, work within the domain of evolutionary psychology that is conducted by scholars who are interested in helping us understand human nature, simply has no conceptual and/or empirical overlap with eugenics whatsoever.

SUMMARY: EVOLUTIONARY PSYCHOLOGY IS REALLY NOT EVIL!

Shrouded in controversy, evolutionary psychology has often run into resistance from angles across the political spectrum. From the political right, religious fundamentalists have expressed concerns about this perspective based on its ideas regarding the nature of human origins. From the far political left, evolutionary psychology has encountered resistance regarding claims that this perspective espouses a genetically deterministic view of human nature.

Perhaps the largest controversy in the field pertains to the idea of evolved behavioral sex differences in humans—an issue that sparks large-scale discussions regarding the idea of men and women being naturally different from one another in certain ways. An additional controversy pertains to the idea of genetic determinism, or what it means for genes to affect behavior. Further, concerns have been raised regarding the quality of the science employed by evolutionary psychologists as well as the socially concerning notion that evolutionary psychology is a modern form of eugenics. While evolutionary psychologists have made several sharp and coherent statements speaking to these controversial issues, it's clear that having critics raise concerns about this field has the capacity to improve the mission, coherence, and work that characterizes the future of evolutionary psychology.

NOTES

1. Adapted with permission from: Geher, G. (2006a). An evolutionary basis to behavioral differences between cats and dogs? An almost-serious scholarly debate. (Illustrations by Michael Bernier.) *Entelechy: Mind and Culture, 7.* http://www .entelechyjournal.com/glenngeher.html
2. Adapted with permission from: Geher, G., & Gambacorta, D. (2010). Evolution is not relevant to sex differences in humans because I want it that way! Evidence for the politicization of human evolutionary psychology. *EvoS Journal: The Journal of the Evolutionary Studies Consortium, 2*(1), 32–47.
3. Adapted with permission from: Geher, G. (2006b). Evolutionary psychology is not evil . . . and here's why. . . . *Psihologijske Teme (Psychological Topics); Special Issue on Evolutionary Psychology, 15,* 181–202.

DISCUSSION/ESSAY EXERCISES

- Describe the basic idea of *evolved behavioral sex differences*. In your answer, briefly describe how Geher's (2006a) article in *Entelechy* uses metaphors regarding differences between dogs and cats to explore the academic issues at hand. Be sure to address how evolutionary psychologists and social constructionists differentially address issues of how and why males and females behave differently from one another.

- Describe the idea of *genetic determinism* and address how the concepts of *strategic pluralism* and *conditional strategies* relate to this issue. In your answer, address how evolutionary psychologists address this issue using their particular approach to situationism.

- Ketelaar and Ellis (2000) argue that evolutionary psychology provides a coherent meta-theory for understanding all of psychology. Explain how these authors argue that evolutionary psychology is "progressive," leads to novel research questions, and is able to "digest anomalies" in a way that other fields in the behavioral sciences don't.

- Schmitt and Pilcher (2004) provide a clear sense of how we can document evidence for an evolutionary adaptation. Discuss several of the forms of evidence that they describe, and address how research by Profet on pregnancy sickness provides a strong model of how to document evidence of a human behavioral adaptation.

The Future of Evolutionary Psychology

KEY TERMS

- Sociobiology and ethology
- Interest in evolutionary psychology among students
- Interest in evolutionary psychology in the media
- Interest in evolutionary psychology among professors
- Training issues related to evolutionary psychology
- Wilson's three hurdles to evolution education
- Interdisciplinarity and evolutionary psychology
- EvoS

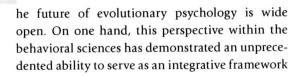

he future of evolutionary psychology is wide open. On one hand, this perspective within the behavioral sciences has demonstrated an unprecedented ability to serve as an integrative framework across the behavioral sciences. As Darwin himself anticipated more than 150 years ago, an evolutionary approach to human behavior has extraordinary potential to shed light on all aspects of human behavior. Evolutionary approaches have been applied to all areas of psychology, including cognitive, developmental, physiological, social, clinical psychology, and more. The idea of human behavior as being ultimately rooted in our evolutionary past has come to greatly advance all areas of psychology.

That said, the application of evolutionary principles to our understanding of issues of humanity is still in its infancy. Given the controversies that have surrounded this approach, attempts to integrate evolution into our understanding of who we are has historically run into stops and starts. While evolutionary psychology has led to extraordinary new insights in all areas of psychology, the resistance met by this field of inquiry continues to be tangible and significant.

INTEREST IN EVOLUTIONARY PSYCHOLOGY

Interest in evolutionary psychology varies as a function of the audience being considered at a particular moment. Undergraduate and graduate students yearn for classes on this topic, as evidenced by the expansion of classes and textbooks in evolutionary psychology across recent years (see Glass, Wilson, and Geher, 2012). Further, interest in evolutionary psychology has been greatly welcomed by the media, showing a disproportionate representation in media sources across the past several years (Garcia et al., 2011). That said, academic institutions continue to push in the other direction, presenting significant resistance to evolutionary psychology on theoretical, methodological, and political grounds (Geher & Gambacorta, 2010).

This dynamic is clearly complex, and it has implications for the future of the field of evolutionary psychology. On one hand, people in general and students in particular are fascinated by this field and are requesting more information on human behavior from this perspective. On the other hand, the halls of academia are quite resistant to the expansion of evolutionary psychology—in spite of student and popular interest in this field (Geher & Gambacorta, 2010). Based on this information alone, the future of this field is murky at best.

HISTORY AND EVOLUTIONARY PSYCHOLOGY

Historically, evolutionary approaches to understanding human behavior have been met with mixed results. While E. O. Wilson's (1975) treatise on evolution and human behavior, found in his renowned book *Sociobiology*, led to great excitement for the idea of evolution playing a major role in helping us understand human behavior, it also led to extraordinary backlash—the point that "sociobiology" is now a questionable word when it comes to publishing anything in the realm of academia.

"Ethology" and other phrases that speak to the idea of evolved behavioral tendencies have, historically, run into similar pockets of controversy (see Geher, 2006a).

Can the idea of understanding human behavior in terms of evolution framed under the rubric of "evolutionary psychology" forge forward where these other attempts have failed? Clearly I hope it can and hope it does. From my perspective, embracing our evolutionary heritage in attempts to understand who we are affords us the best possible opportunity to shed light on the factors underlying human behavior. Modern evolutionary psychology, with an extraordinary amount of empirical work across the behavioral sciences, has extraordinary potential to help advance psychology. Will modern evolutionary psychology fulfill its promise of moving our discipline forward? I hope so.

OBTAINING EDUCATION IN EVOLUTIONARY PSYCHOLOGY

In a recent analysis of factors associated with working in the field of evolutionary psychology, Glass, Wilson, and Geher (2012) reported data on the state of training regarding evolutionary psychology within higher education. In the words of the authors:

> Evolution has famously run into resistance from opponents across the political spectrum. [The data in this research] . . . provide evidence that evolution also runs into dramatic levels of resistance within the academy. To assess this situation, the authors of evolution-themed–articles from the journal *Behavioral and Brain Sciences* between the years 2001 and 2004 were surveyed regarding the state of evolutionary training at their previous and current institutions. The respondents indicated, on the whole, that their graduate school education had focused little on general evolution and even less on evolution as applied to human behavior. Further, much of their own evolutionary knowledge was self-taught and self-initiated—and they generally believed that students or faculty at their current institutions would have difficulty receiving evolutionary training.
>
> In short, based on information obtained from the top researchers in the field of evolutionary psychology, we found the following:

- It was difficult for these scholars to obtain training on studying the interface of evolution and human behavior in their own graduate training.
- These scholars believe that students at their current institutions would not easily be able to learn about the principles of evolutionary psychology.

- These scholars largely felt that they had to train themselves regarding the principles of evolutionary psychology.
- These scholars believe that other scholars at their universities would find it difficult to obtain a strong education regarding evolutionary psychology. (p. 16)

Think about the implications of this research! On one hand, evolutionary psychology has arrived, leading to a high prevalence of publications in a major peer-reviewed journal in the behavioral sciences. On the other hand, the primary authors of these articles report having had to go out of their way to learn about the principles of evolutionary psychology—and paint a bleak picture regarding the future of education in this field for others.

THE PRACTICAL UTILITY OF EVOLUTION IN EVERYDAY LIFE

David Sloan Wilson's (2007) now-classic book, *Evolution for Everyone*, is largely designed to expose a broad audience to the basic principles of evolution, and to help assuage concerns that many people have regarding this approach to understanding the nature of life. In this book, Wilson talks about three basic hurdles to evolution education:

1. People believe that evolution is rooted in science, and science is too difficult to understand.
2. People believe that evolution is not relevant to everyday life.
3. People believe that evolution is probably evil.

These summaries of Wilson's points speak to clear and palpable hurdles regarding the future of evolutionary psychology. In fact, the basic ideas of evolution—and natural selection in particular—are not that complex. A phobia of science is generally unhealthy, and conflating this phobia with an understanding of evolution is really not necessary. Evolution is simply the idea that replicating entities outcompete nonreplicating entities across time.

Hopefully, by this point, you can see that evolutionary psychology is highly relevant to many aspects of everyday life. From one's emotional state to one's relationship status to one's health, evolution has substantial relevance. Seeing the practical implications of evolution will surely be a catalyst for facilitating the growth of evolutionary psychology in the future.

Finally, I hope that this book provides sufficient information regarding the idea that evolutionary psychology is somehow *evil*. Any and all sets of intellectual ideas can be used for antisocial or prosocial purposes. Evolutionary psychology is, at its core, the application of ideas from the most powerful theory in the life sciences to issues of human behavior. There is nothing inherently evil about this endeavor and, in fact, this approach to understanding who we are can be a tool used for good purposes!

EVOLUTIONARY PSYCHOLOGY AND EVOLUTIONARY STUDIES

While traditional academic departments may not always welcome evolutionary approaches (see Glass et al., 2012), interdisciplinary approaches to higher education, which are often touted as representing the future of higher education, may well foster the future growth of evolutionary psychology.

Based on several objective indices, evolutionary psychology is a relatively interdisciplinary academic endeavor (see Chang, Geher, Waldo, & Wilson, 2011; Garcia et al., 2011; & Geher, Crosier, Dillon, & Chang, 2011). Evolutionary psychologists draw on the expertise of colleagues across academic disciplines, often collaborating with scholars from outside traditional psychology departments.

Modern academic institutions have recently started to focus efforts on the pedagogical importance of interdisciplinary approaches to higher education (see Garcia et al., 2011). As an exemplar of this approach, SUNY Binghamton and New Paltz have taken the lead in starting interdisciplinary evolutionary studies (EvoS) programs—with students taking courses across multiple disciplines, such as anthropology, biology, English, geology, and psychology, all with a focus on how evolution can tie together academic areas of inquiry and connect disparate phenomena, such as why Devonian fossils take the form that they do or why Shakespeare's work so often focuses on issues of power and sex.

In such a dynamic interdisciplinary kind of program (which, by the way, has received hundreds of thousands of dollars from the National Science Foundation), evolutionary psychology is a powerful, important, and central element of the curriculum.

If the future of higher education moves in the direction of interdisciplinarity, as many administrators within academic circles indicate, evolutionary psychology may well have a fighting chance! Again, the future is, as always, uncertain. But given the powerful work done in recent years by evolutionary psychologists coupled with trends toward interdisciplinarity in higher education, the future of evolutionary psychology may well be very bright.

SUMMARY: EVOLUTIONARY PSYCHOLOGY IN A CRYSTAL BALL

Evolutionary psychology has had a rocky history—and its future is necessarily unclear. Past efforts to advance approaches to human behavior based on evolutionary principles have met with mixed success.

In the modern state of academia, evolutionary psychology has led to many successes, including achieving popularity among students and the media. However, resistance to this field within the halls of modern academia is palpable—a fact that makes the future of evolutionary psychology necessarily unclear.

That said, academia seems to be moving toward a relatively interdisciplinary approach in curricula offerings. Given the highly interdisciplinary approach that characterizes evolutionary psychology, this fact may bode well for the future of this field. Evolutionary psychology has demonstrated itself to be practical and powerful in its explanatory power. While the future of this field within academia is necessarily uncertain, the cultivation of evolutionary psychology is certain to help shed important light on issues of humanity.

DISCUSSION/ESSAY EXERCISES

- Briefly describe issues regarding degree of interest in evolutionary psychology among students, the media, and professors. In your description, address points of conflict of interest, and discuss how this conflict of interest relates to the future of evolutionary psychology.
- Describe Glass, Wilson, and Geher's (2012) work on training related to evolutionary psychology. In your answer, describe evidence relating to how advanced evolutionary psychology is—along with hurdles that exist regarding the training of future evolutionary psychologists.
- Describe the idea of *interdisciplinarity* along with modern trends in interdisciplinarity in higher education. Related to this point, address the issue of "evolutionary psychology's relatively interdisciplinary nature." Finally, address how, taken together, these points make a case for a positive future for evolutionary psychology within modern academia.

References

Ainsworth, M., Blehar, M. C., Waters, E., & Wall, S. (1978). *Patterns of attachment: A psychological study of the strange situation.* Hillsdale, NJ: Erlbaum.

Anderson, K. G. (2006). How well does paternity confidence match actual paternity? *Current Anthropology, 47,* 513–520.

Applied Evolutionary Psychology Society. Retrieved January 18, 2013, from http://www.aepsociety.org

Axelrod, R. (1984). *The evolution of cooperation.* New York, NY: Basic Books.

Barclay, P. (2011). Competitive helping increases with the size of biological markets and invades defection. *Journal of Theoretical Biology, 281,* 47–55.

Belsky, J. (1997). Attachment, mating and parenting: An evolutionary interpretation. *Human Nature, 8,* 361–381.

Bingham, P., & Souza, J. (2009). *Death from a distance and the birth of a humane universe: Human evolution, behavior, history, and your future.* New York, NY: BookSurge Publications.

Bingham, P. M., & Souza, J. (2012). Ultimate causation in evolved human political psychology: Implications for public policy. *Journal of Social, Evolutionary, and Cultural Psychology, 6,* 360–383.

Bouchard, T. (2007). Genes and human psychological traits. In P. Carruthers, S. Laurence, & S. Stich (Eds.), *The innate mind: Foundations for the future.* Oxford, UK: Oxford University Press.

Bowlby, J. (1969). *Attachment and loss: Vol. 1. Attachment.* New York, NY: Basic Books.

Buller, D. (2005). Evolutionary psychology: The emperor's new paradigm. *Trends in Cognitive Science, 9,* 277–283.

Burnstein, E. (2005). Altruism and genetic relatedness. In D. M. Buss (Ed.), *The handbook of evolutionary psychology.* New York, NY: Wiley.

Buss, D. (1989). Sex differences in human mate preferences: Evolutionary hypotheses tested in 37 cultures. *Behavioral and Brain Sciences, 12,* 1–49.

Buss, D. M. (2003). *The evolution of desire: Strategies of human mating.* New York, NY: Basic Books.

Buss, D. M. (2005). *The murderer next door: Why the mind is designed to kill.* New York, NY: Penguin.

Buss, D. M., Abbott, M., Angleitner, A., Biaggio, A., Blanco-Villasenor, A., & Bruchon-Schweitzer, M. (1990). International preferences in selecting mates: A study of 37 societies. *Journal of Cross-Cultural Psychology, 21,* 5–47.

Buss, D. M., & Haselton, M. G. (2005). The evolution of jealousy: A reply to Buller. *Trends in Cognitive Science, 9,* 506–507.

Buss, D. M., Larsen, R. J., Westen, D., & Semmelroth, J. (1992). Sex differences in jealousy: Evolution, physiology and psychology. *Psychological Science, 3,* 251–255.

Buss, D. M., & Schmitt, D. P. (1993). Sexual strategies theory: An evolutionary perspective on human mating. *Psychological Review, 100,* 204–232.

Chang, R., Geher, G., Waldo, J., & Wilson, D. S. (Eds.). (2011). Special issue on the EvoS Consortium. *Evolution: Education & Outreach, 4.*

Clark, R. D. & Hatfield, E. (1989). Gender differences in receptivity to sexual offers. *Journal of Psychology and Human Sexuality, 2,* 39–55.

Cordain, L. (2010). *The paleo diet: Lose weight and get healthy by eating the foods you were designed to eat.* New York, NY: Wiley.

Cosmides, L., & Tooby, J. (1997). The modular nature of human intelligence. In A. B. Scheibel & J. W. Schopf (Eds.), *The origin and evolution of intelligence.* Sudbury, MA: Jones & Bartlett.

Costa, P. T., & McCrae, R. R. (1992). *The revised NEO personality inventory and NEO five-factor inventory manual.* Odessa, FL: Psychological Assessment Resources.

Cunningham, M. R. (1986). Measuring the physical in physical attractiveness: Quasi-experiments on the sociobiology of female facial beauty. *Journal of Personality and Social Psychology, 50,* 925–935.

Daly, M., & Wilson, M. (1988). *Homicide.* New York, NY: Aldine de Gruyter.

Daly, M., Wilson, M., & Weghorst, S. J. (1982). Male sexual jealousy. *Ethology and Sociobiology, 3,* 11–27.

Darke, R. (2002). *The American woodland garden: Capturing the spirit of the deciduous forest.* Portland, OR: Timber Press.

Darwin, C. (1859). *On the origin of species by means of natural selection, or the preservation of favoured races in the struggle for life* (1st ed.). London, UK: John Murray.

Darwin, C. (1871). *The descent of man, and selection in relation to sex* (2 vols.). London, UK: John Murray.

Darwin, C. (1872). *The expression of the emotions in man and animals.* London, UK: John Murray.

Dawkins, R. (1976). *The selfish gene.* Oxford, UK: Oxford University Press.

Dawkins, R. (2005). Afterword to D. M. Buss (Ed.), *The handbook of evolutionary psychology.* New York, NY: Wiley.

Dawkins, R. (2006). *The god delusion.* Boston, MA: Houghton Mifflin.

de Waal, F. B. (1989). *Peacemaking among primates.* Cambridge, MA: Harvard University Press.

Dunbar, R. I. M. (1992). Neocortex size as a constraint on group size in primates. *Journal of Human Evolution, 20,* 469–493.

Dutton, D. (2010). *The art instinct: Beauty, pleasure, and human evolution.* New York, NY: Bloomsbury Press.

Egan, J. (2006, March 19). Wanted: A few good sperm. *New York Times Magazine.* Retrieved August 20, 2013, from http://www.nytimes.com/2006/03/19/magazine/319dad.html?pagewanted=all&_r=0

Ekman, P., & Friesen, W. V. (1968). Nonverbal behavior in psychotherapy research. In J. Shlien (Ed.), *Research in psychotherapy* (Vol. 3) (pp. 179–216). Washington, DC: American Psychological Association.

Figueredo, A. J., Brumbach, B. H., Jones, D. N., Sefcek, J. A., Vasquez, G., & Jacobs, W. J. (2008). Ecological constraints on mating tactics. In G. Geher & G. Miller (Eds.), *Mating intelligence: Sex, relationships, and the mind's reproductive system* (pp. 337–365). Mahwah, NJ: Lawrence Erlbaum.

Fisher, H. (2004). *Why we love: The nature and chemistry of romantic love.* New York, NY: Holt.

Fisher, M., Cox, A., & Gordon, F. (2009). Deciding between competition derogation and self-promotion. *Journal of Evolutionary Psychology, 7,* 287–308.

Fisher, M. L., Geher, G., Cox, A., Tran, U. S., Hoben, A., Arrabaca, A., . . . Voracek, M. (2009). Impact of relational proximity on distress from infidelity. *Evolutionary Psychology, 7,* 560–580.

Fiske, S. T., & Taylor, S. E. (1990). *Social cognition*. Reading, MA: Addison-Wesley.

Gallup, G., Burch, R. L., & Berens Mitchell, T. J. (2006). Semen displacement as a sperm competition strategy: Multiple mating, self-semen displacement, and timing in-pair copulations. *Human Nature, 17*, 253–264.

Gallup, G., Burch, R. L., Zappieri, M. L., Parvez, R. A., Stockwell, M. L., & Davis, J. A. (2003). The human penis as a semen displacement device. *Evolution and Human Behavior, 24*, 277–289.

Gallup, G. G., & Frederick, D. A. (2010). The science of sex appeal: An evolutionary perspective. *Review of General Psychology, 14*, 240–250.

Gangestad, S. W., & Simpson, J. A. (2000). The evolution of human mating: Trade-offs and strategic pluralism. *Behavioral and Brain Sciences, 23*, 573–587.

Gangestad, S. W., & Thornhill, R. (1998). Menstrual cycle variation in women's preferences for the scent of symmetrical men. *Proceedings of the Royal Society of London* B, *265*, 927–933.

Gangestad, S. W., Thornhill, R., & Garver-Apgar, C. E. (2005). Adaptations to ovulation: Implications for sexual and social behavior. *Current Directions in Psychological Science, 14*, 312–316.

Garcia, J. R., Geher, G., Crosier, B., Saad, G., Gambacorta, D., Johnsen, L., & Pranckitas, E. (2011). The interdisciplinary context of evolutionary approaches to human behavior: A key to survival in the ivory archipelago. *Futures, 43*, 749–761.

Garvey, K. J., Brosseau, K., & Jennings, P. (2012). *The reverse trolley dilemma: Utilitarian vs. deontological moral judgments*. Presentation at the 6th annual meeting of the NorthEastern Evolutionary Psychology Society, Plymouth, NH.

Geher, G. (2006a). An evolutionary basis to behavioral differences between cats and dogs? An almost-serious scholarly debate. *Entelechy: Mind and Culture*, spring/summer, No. 7.

Geher, G. (2006b). Evolutionary psychology is not evil . . . and here's why. . . . *Psihologijske Teme (Psychological Topics); Special Issue on Evolutionary Psychology, 2*, 181–202.

Geher, G. (2009). Accuracy and oversexualization in cross-sex mind-reading: An adaptationist approach. *Evolutionary Psychology, 7*, 331–347.

Geher, G. (2011). Evolutionarily informed parenting: A ripe area for scholarship in evolutionary studies. *EvoS Journal: The Journal of the Evolutionary Studies Consortium, 3*(2), 26–36.

Geher, G., Camargo, M. A., & O'Rourke, S. (2008). Future directions in research on mating intelligence. In G. Geher & G. F. Miller (Eds.), *Mating intelligence: Sex, relationships, and the mind's reproductive system.* Mahwah, NJ: Lawrence Erlbaum Associates.

Geher, G., Crosier, B., Dillon, H. M., & Chang, R. (2011). Evolutionary psychology's place in evolutionary studies: A tale of promise and challenge. *Evolution: Education & Outreach, 4,* 11–16. Special issue on EvoS Consortium (R. Chang, G. Geher, J. Waldo, & D. S. Wilson, Eds.).

Geher, G., & Gambacorta, D. (2010). Evolution is not relevant to sex differences in humans because I want it that way! Evidence for the politicization of human evolutionary psychology. *EvoS Journal: The Journal of the Evolutionary Studies Consortium, 2,* 32–47.

Geher, G., & Kaufman, S. B. (2013). *Mating intelligence unleashed: The role of the mind in sex, dating, and love.* New York, NY: Oxford University Press.

Geher, G., & Miller, G. F. (Eds.). (2008). *Mating intelligence: Sex, relationships, and the mind's reproductive system.* Mahwah, NJ: Lawrence Erlbaum Associates.

Glass, D. J. (2012). Evolutionary clinical psychology, broadly construed: Perspectives on obsessive-compulsive disorder. *Journal of Social, Evolutionary, and Cultural Psychology, 6,* 292–308.

Glass, D. J., Wilson, D. S., & Geher, G. (2012). Evolutionary training in relation to human affairs is sorely lacking in higher education. *EvoS Journal: The Journal of the Evolutionary Studies Consortium, 4,* 16–22.

Gould, S. J. (1980). *The panda's thumb.* New York, NY: W. W. Norton.

Gray, P. (2011). The special value of age-mixed play. *American Journal of Play, 3,* 500–522.

Grey, J. (1992). *Men Are from Mars, Women Are from Venus.* New York, NY: Harper Collins.

Gross, M. R. (1982). Sneakers, satellites, and parentals: Polymorphic mating strategies in North American sunfishes. *Zeitschrift fur Tierpsychologie, 60,* 1–26.

Hamilton, W. D. (1964). The genetical evolution of social behaviour. *Journal of Theoretical Biology, 7,* 1–16.

Haselton, M. G., & Miller, G. F. (2006). Women's fertility across the cycle increases the short-term attractiveness of creative intelligence compared to wealth. *Human Nature, 17,* 50–73.

Hobbs, D., & Gallup, G. (2011). Songs as a medium for embedded reproductive messages. *Evolutionary Psychology, 9,* 390–416.

Hodgson, J. A., Bergey, C. M., & Disotell, T. R. (2010). Neanderthal genome: The ins and outs of African genetic diversity. *Current Biology, 20,* 517–519.

Hrdy, S. B. (2009) *Mothers and others: The evolutionary origins of mutual understanding.* Cambridge, MA: Harvard University Press.

Hughes, A. L. (1988). *Evolution and human kinship.* New York, NY: Oxford University Press.

Hughes, S., Harrison, M., & Gallup, G. (2004). Sex differences in mating and multiple concurrent sex partners *Sexualities, Evolution, and Gender, 6,* 3–13.

Hughes, S., Harrison, M., & Gallup, G. (2007). Sex differences in kissing among college students. *Evolutionary Psychology, 5,* 612–631.

Johnsen, L. L., Kruger, D. J., & Geher, G. (2011). *Childhood injuries as an early practice of intra-sexual competition.* Oral presentation given at the meeting of the NorthEastern Evolutionary Psychology Society, Binghamton, NY.

Keller, M. C., & Nesse, R. M. (2006). The evolutionary significance of depressive symptoms: Different life events lead to different depressive symptom patterns. *Journal of Personality and Social Psychology, 91,* 316–330.

Ketelaar, T., & Ellis, B. J. (2000). Are evolutionary explanations unfalsifiable? Evolutionary psychology and the Lakatosian philosophy of science. *Psychological Inquiry, 11,* 1–21.

Kissinger, H. (1973, October 28). *New York Times.* http://select.nytimes.com/gst/abstract.html?res=F00F1FF73D55137B93C4AB178BD95F478785F9

Kramare, C., & Treichler, P. A. (1996). *A feminist dictionary.* Champaign, IL: University of Illinois Press.

Kruger, D. J., Fisher, M., & Jobling, I. (2003). Proper and dark heroes as dads and cads: Alternative mating strategies in British Romantic literature. *Human Nature, 14,* 305–317.

Kruger, D. J., & Nesse, R. M. (2007). Economic transition, male competition, and sex differences in mortality rates. *Evolutionary Psychology, 5,* 411–427.

Kurzban, R. (2010). *Why everyone (else) is a hypocrite: Evolution and the modular mind*. Princeton, NJ: Princeton University Press.

Kurzban, R., & Haselton, M. G. (2005). Making hay out of straw: Real and imagined debates in evolutionary psychology. In J. Barkow (Ed.), *Missing the revolution: Darwinism for social scientists*. New York, NY: Oxford University Press.

Li, N. P. (2008). Intelligent priorities. In G. Geher & G. F. Miller (Eds.), *Mating intelligence: Sex, relationships, and the mind's reproduction system* (pp. 105–120). Mahwah, NJ: Lawrence Erlbaum Associates.

Lorenz, K. (1963). *On aggression*. Austria: Methuen Publishing.

Low, B. S. (1990). Marriage systems and pathogen stress in human societies. *American Zoologist, 30*, 325–339.

Marchant, S., & Higgins, P. J. (1990). *Handbook of Australian, New Zealand and Antarctic birds, Vol. 1A*. Melbourne, AU: Oxford University Press.

Maynard Smith, J. (2002). *Evolutionary genetics*. New York, NY: Oxford University Press.

Miller, G. F. (2000). *The mating mind: How sexual choice shaped the evolution of human nature*. New York, NY: Doubleday.

Miller, G. F. (2007). Sexual selection for moral virtues. *Quarterly Review of Biology, 82*, 97–125.

Miller, G. F., Tybur, J., & Jordan, B. (2007). Ovulatory cycle effects on tip earnings by lap-dancers: Economic evidence for human estrus? *Evolution and Human Behavior, 28*, 375–381.

Nelson, H., & Geher, G. (2007). Mutual grooming in human dyadic relationships: An ethological perspective. *Current Psychology, 26*, 121–140.

Nettle, D., & Clegg, H. (2006). Schizotypy, creativity and mating success in humans. *Proceedings of the Royal Society: B, 273*, 611–615.

Nettle, D., & Clegg, H. (2008). Personality, mating strategies, and mating intelligence. In G. Geher & G. Miller (Eds.), *Mating intelligence: Sex, relationships, and the mind's reproductive system* (pp. 121–135). New York, NY: Lawrence Erlbaum.

O'Brien, D., Geher, G., Gallup, A. C., Garcia, J. R., & Kaufman, S. B. (2010). Self-perceived mating intelligence predicts sexual behavior in college students: Empirical validation of a theoretical construct. *Imagination, Cognition, and Personality, 29*, 341–362.

O'Sullivan, M. (2008). Deception and self-deception as strategies in short- and long-term mating. In G. Geher & G. F. Miller (Eds.),

Mating intelligence: Sex, relationships, and the mind's reproduction system. Mahwah, NJ: Lawrence Erlbaum Associates.

Packer, C., & Pusey, A. E. (1983). Adaptations of female lions to infanticide by incoming males. *The American Naturalist, 121*, 716–728.

Perrill, S. A., Gerhardt, H. C., & Daniel, R. (1978). Sexual parasitism in the green tree frog (Holy cinerea). *Science, 200*, 1179–1180.

Peterson, A., Geher, G., & Kaufman, S. B. (2011). Predicting preferences for sex acts: Which traits matter and why? *Evolutionary Psychology, 9*, 371–389.

Pinker, S. (1999). *How the mind works*. New York, NY: W.W. Norton & Company.

Pinker, S. (2003). *The blank slate: The modern denial of human nature*. New York, NY: Penguin.

Pinker, S. (2012). *The better angels of our nature: Why violence has declined*. New York, NY: Penguin.

Pipitone, R. N. & Gallup, G. G., Jr. (2008). Women's voice attractiveness varies across the menstrual cycle. *Evolution and Human Behavior, 29*, 268–274.

Platek, S., Geher, G., Heywood, L., Stapell, H., Porter, R., & Waters, T. (2011). Walking the walk to teach the talk: Implementing ancestral lifestyle changes as the newest tool in evolutionary studies. *Evolution: Education and Outreach, 4*, 41–51. Special issue on EvoS Consortium (R. Chang, G. Geher, J. Waldo, & D. S. Wilson, Eds.).

Platek, S. M., Burch, R. L., Panyavin, I. S., Wasserman, B. H., & Gallup, G. (2002). Reactions to children's faces: Resemblance affects males more than females. *Evolution and Human Behavior, 23*, 159–166.

Platek, S. M., & Singh, D. (2010). Optimal waist-to-hip ratios in women activate neural reward centers in men. *PLoS ONE 5*: e9042.

Popper, K. R. (1994). Zwei Bedeutungen von Falsifizierbarkeit [Two meanings of falsifiability]. In H. Seiffert & G. Radnitzky, *Handlexikon der Wissenschaftstheorie* (pp. 82–85). München: Deutscher Taschenbuch Verlag.

Profet, M. (1988). The evolution of pregnancy sickness as protection to the embryo against Pleistocene teratogens. *Evolutionary Theory, 8*, 177–190.

Robinson, L. J., & Ferrier, I. N. (2006). Evolution of cognitive impairment in bipolar disorder: A systematic review of cross-sectional evidence. *Bipolar Disorders, 8*, 103–116.

Ross, L., & Nisbett, R.E. (1991). *The person and the situation: Perspectives of social psychology.* New York, NY: McGraw Hill.

Schlaepfer, M. A., Runge, M. C., & Sherman, P. W. (2002). Ecological and evolutionary traps. *Trends in Ecology and Evolution, 17*, 474–480.

Schmitt, D. P. (2008). Attachment matters: Patterns of romantic attachment across gender, geography, and cultural forms. In J. P. Forgas & J. Fitness (Eds.), *Social relationships: Cognitive, affective, and motivational processes* (pp. 75–97). New York, NY: Psychology Press.

Schmitt, D. P., & Pilcher, J. J. (2004). Evaluating evidence of psychological adaptation: How do we know one when we see one? *Psychological Science, 15*, 643–649.

Schmitt, D. P., et al. (2004). Patterns and universals of mate poaching across 53 nations: The effects of sex, culture, and personality on romantically attracting another person's partner. *Journal of Personality and Social Psychology, 86*, 560–584.

Sherman, P. W. (1985). Alarm calls of Belding's ground squirrels to aerial predators: Nepotism or self-preservation? *Behavioral Ecology and Sociobiology, 17*, 313–323.

Simpson, J. A., & Gangestad, S. W. (1991). Individual differences in sociosexuality: Convergent and discriminant validation. *Journal of Personality and Social Psychology, 60*, 870–883.

Singh, D., & Singh, D. (2006). Role of body fat and body shape on judgment of female health and attractiveness: An evolutionary perspective. *Psychological Topics, 2*, 331–350.

Smith, D. L. (2007). *The most dangerous animal.* New York, NY: St. Marten's Press.

Tajfel, H. (1981). *Human groups and social categories.* Cambridge, UK: Cambridge University Press.

Tinbergen, N. (1963). On aims and methods of ethology. *Zeitschrift für Tierpsychologie, 20*, 410–433.

Trivers, R. L. (1971). The evolution of reciprocal altruism. *The Quarterly Review of Biology, 46*, 35–57.

Trivers, R. L. (1972). Parental investment and sexual selection. In B. Campbell (Ed.), *Sexual selection and the descent of man: 1871–1971* (pp. 136–179). Chicago, IL: Aldine.

Trivers, R. L. (1974). Parent-offspring conflict. *American Zoologist, 14*, 249–264.

Trivers, R. L. (1985) *Social evolution.* Menlo Park, CA: Benjamin/Cummings.

Wason, P. (1966). Reasoning. In B. M. Foss (Ed.), *New horizons in psychology*. London, UK: Penguin.

Wilkinson, G. S. (1984). Reciprocal food sharing in the vampire bat. *Nature, 308*, 181–184.

Williams, G. C. (1966). *Adaptation and natural selection*. Princeton, NJ: Princeton University Press.

Wilson, D. S. (2002). *Darwin's cathedral: Evolution, religion and the nature of society*. Chicago, IL: University of Chicago Press.

Wilson, D. S. (2007). *Evolution for everyone: How Darwin's theory can change the way we think about our lives*. New York, NY: Delacorte Press.

Wilson, D. S. (2011). *The neighborhood project: Using evolution to improve my city one block at a time*. New York, NY: Little, Brown, and Company.

Wilson, D. S., Dietrich, E., & Clark, A. (2003). On the inappropriate use of the naturalistic fallacy in evolutionary psychology. *Biology and Philosophy, 18*, 669–682.

Wilson, E. O. (1975). *Sociobiology*. Cambridge, MA: Harvard University Press.

Wilson, M., & Daly, M. (1985). Competitiveness, risk-taking and violence: The young male syndrome. *Ethology and Sociobiology, 6*, 59–73.

Wolf, R. (2010). *The paleo solution: The original human diet*. Las Vegas, NV: Victory Belt.

Woolfenden, G. E., & Fitzpatrick, J. W. (1984). *The Florida scrub jay: Demography of a cooperative breeding bird*. Princeton, NJ: Princeton University Press.

Wrangham, R. (2010). *Catching fire: How cooking made us human*. New York, NY: Basic Books.

Zahavi, A. (1975). Mate selection—A selection for a handicap. *Journal of Theoretical Biology, 53*, 205–214.

Index